TAKE ACTION!

How to Meet Women and Get Dates

By Kenneth Scott

Published by:

Personal Development Publishing
Post Office Box 27424
Houston, Texas 77227, USA
mail@dating-pickup-lines.com
www.dating-pickup-lines.com

Copyright © 2004, by Personal Development Publishing
Printed in the United States of America

Library of Congress Control Number: 2004107743

Publisher's Cataloging-in-Publication Data

Scott, Kenneth, 1967-
    Take Action! : How to Meet Women and Get Dates/ by Kenneth Scott – 1st ed.
    p. cm.
    LCCN 2004107743
    ISBN 0-9755914-0-1

    1. Dating (Social customs) 2. Man-woman relationships.   I. Title

HQ801.S4413 2004   646.7'7
                           QBI04-200260

For my beautiful wife –

Without your support and encouragement
this book would never have been possible.

Table of Contents

Introduction

Imagine yourself at a coffee shop reading the newspaper and sipping a latte on a Saturday morning. Suddenly in walks this incredibly gorgeous woman. While she is in line you notice her left hand and, as luck would have it, she is not wearing a ring. She gets her coffee, sits at a table near you and begins reading a book.

So what do you do? If you are like most men, absolutely nothing. You might check her out, making sure to avert your eyes if she caught you looking. But as far as anything that might actually lead to meeting her or getting her phone number or getting a date with her, you do absolutely nothing. Eventually she leaves and you never see her again.

What if you were a different kind of man? The kind who could confidently approach a woman and introduce himself. The kind who could strike up a conversation and ask for her number. You can become that man if you follow the ideas and principles described in this book. You can take charge of your life and have a great time meeting women and getting dates.

In a nutshell, here is what you can expect to learn from this book: how to approach any woman in almost any situation, strike up a conversation with her, and ask her for her phone number. This is not a book about relationships or about how to get a woman to fall in love with you. The sole focus is to help you get more dates with the women you **really** want to date.

My personal story is not that unusual. I dated women I met at work or school and a few turned into serious girlfriends. But I never developed the ability to approach a girl without knowing her or being introduced to her. Like most men, my fear of rejection kept me from ever attempting something as bold as approaching a stranger.

For most men it is impossible to get past their fear of rejection without some significant motivation. For me, that motivation came in the form of being unceremoniously dumped by a girlfriend I had lived with for two years.

I was devastated. I found myself alone, about 20 pounds overweight, unenthusiastic about my career, and generally very unhappy. It embarrasses me to think about it now, but at the time I wondered how I would ever find someone to date. I felt like I had hit rock bottom.

The good thing about hitting rock bottom is that you have no place to go but up. Motivated by anger I became obsessed with getting back in shape. Very quickly, I was able to do just that.

But I had another, much bigger problem. I had absolutely no confidence with women. It had been nearly three years since I had asked a woman out on a date and I just could not picture myself doing it.

I knew that I could not be the first man to have felt this way. In fact, I knew intuitively that most men feel exactly this way most of the time. But I had also known a few guys who seemed very comfortable with women, even women they had just met. These men had something I wanted – the ability to approach beautiful women. So I began to research the subject, hoping that someone had written something that would help me to become one of these men.

Fortunately, my research turned up quite a bit of material and I devoured it. Some of the information was very helpful, some of it was kind of cheesy, and some of it was just plain bad advice.

Throughout my research, and my own personal experience, several recurrent themes began to appear. First, if you want to succeed with women you need to have some courage and deal with your fear of rejection. Second, when meeting a girl you should focus less on trying to impress her and focus more on her. In other words, talk less about yourself and more about her. Third, and most importantly, confidence is incredibly attractive to women.

If you follow the advice in this book you will drastically improve your ability to meet women and get dates.

14 –Take Action!

Chapter One

Understanding Women

A. The Survey

In preparing to write this book I realized that it was important to rely not only on my own experiences, but also to go directly to the source. To find out what women thought about the subject. So I conducted a survey of fifty attractive single women in their twenties or thirties. I wanted to know what they thought about men approaching them, how they felt about giving out their phone numbers, what they found attractive in a man, and what they thought about a variety of other issues. Their answers were both interesting and encouraging. The actual survey that was distributed is attached in the Appendix along with a summary of the responses.

B. How do Women Feel About Being Approached?

The most significant piece of information came in response to the very first question. Women were asked whether men "should be bolder about approaching women." The response was overwhelming: **82% thought that men should be bolder.**

As men, this needs to be drilled into our heads. Women want us to approach them. They want to feel special and appreciated. Repeat this to yourself over and over until it is embedded in your brain.

Think about it from a typical girl's point of view. Before she leaves in the morning she spends a lot of time getting ready – fixing her hair, putting on makeup, picking out the right outfit, etc. When you approach her and show interest she will feel flattered and good about herself. How could she not appreciate a guy who appreciates her?

The survey also asked women to identify those places where they would be most open to being approached. Significantly, the responses showed that most women are open to being approached almost anywhere. Of the twenty places listed, at least half of the women said that fourteen were appropriate places to meet. And even the other six got quite a few "yes" responses. The clear message from the responses was that women want men to approach them and where this happens is unimportant.

C. What do Women Want to Hear When You Approach Them?

The survey asked the women what a man should say if he wanted to meet them. They responded as follows:

Say something funny	38%
Make idle chit chat	32%
Give a compliment	22%
Pretend he knows you	8%

There is no clear consensus on exactly what you should say, but the top two answers involve creating a relaxed atmosphere when you first approach. In other words, keep it loose and relaxed.

It is interesting that the top answer was to say something funny. It should come as no surprise that women like a man with a good sense of humor. But before you start memorizing a bunch of knock-knock jokes, think about what this means.

From talking with women, I believe what they really mean is that they like a guy to have a relaxed, lighthearted attitude. It says he is confident and comfortable with himself, both of which are very sexy qualities to women. So, you do not need to walk up and say "Hi. A priest, a rabbi, and a duck walk into a bar together . . ." Just smile at her and be yourself.

Some of the responses to the narrative questions were also very instructive. First, when asked to describe the best approach a man had ever used on them, most had very little to say, some nothing at all. There were a few descriptions of a guy using a joke, most often in a bar. But most of the women had no real story to tell. In other words, most of the women surveyed had never had a man approach them in any kind of memorable way. And a lot of these girls were **very** good looking.

This explains why you can make such an impression on a girl by being bold and approaching her. No matter how beautiful a girl may be she is not approached as frequently as you might imagine. She might get hit on at bars or occasionally asked out by guys she knows at work or school, but women rarely encounter a man who is courageous enough to approach them without some kind of introduction. You can really set yourself apart by being that bold.

Another interesting set of narrative responses came to the question about the worst approaches a girl had ever experienced. Unlike the question about best approaches, most of the women did have an answer to this question. They described approaches ranging from cheesy to downright criminal. Everything from vulgar questions ("do you have a mirror in your pocket because I can see myself in your pants") to literally having their butts grabbed by a complete stranger. The impression I got was that a lot of these were drunk guys in a bar.

The bottom line to what you should say when you approach a woman is that your attitude and confidence are actually a lot more important than the words that you say.

D. How Do Women Evaluate a Man's Physical Attractiveness?

The survey asked the women to list, in order of importance, five factors that are used as criteria for evaluating a man's physical attractiveness. The ranking, in order from most important to least important, was:

1.   handsome face
2.   grooming
3.   well dressed
tie-4. height
tie-4. good body

It is significant to note how high grooming and clothes ranked. This reinforces just how important these factors are to women and how you can greatly improve your attractiveness by dressing well and keeping yourself well groomed.

It is not surprising that women would rank facial attractiveness high. Everyone wants to go out with someone they find attractive. But it is important to remember that women have a much broader definition of "attractive" than men do. It is also much harder to predict. A girl might find a particular guy unattractive while another girl might consider the same guy gorgeous because he had blue eyes or olive skin or whatever particular trait it is that she liked. Or, even more likely, a girl might not think much about a guy's looks and then, after he makes it clear that he is interested in her, she begins to see him differently and becomes more attracted to him.

I went to school with a very cute girl who had a big crush on a classmate who had this big scar on his face. Most of the other girls thought he was unattractive because of the scar, but she thought it was sexy. Not only did she not find the scar unattractive, it was actually the reason she found him attractive. This just illustrates how different women can find different things attractive in a man.

The narrative responses to the question of "what makes a man sexy/attractive" were also very instructive. The responses essentially said that women absolutely love confident men, men who are not scared of them, who are bold and willing to approach them. They simply love men who are sure of themselves.

E. How Do Women Feel About Giving Out Their Phone Number?

When men meet women they are often nervous about asking for a phone number. We will discuss how to handle this in detail in Chapter 10, but it is important to understand that women are a lot less bothered about giving out their number than you might think.

The survey asked women what they would be most likely to do if they were interested in a man they had just met. Their responses were:

66%	Give him my cell or home number
26%	Get his number or email address
8%	Give him my email address

Clearly most women are not concerned about giving out their phone number if they become interested in a guy, even if they just met. So don't be afraid to ask.

Certainly you will come across girls who are a little reluctant since you just met, but even these girls are willing to get your information. Obviously, it is better if you have her contact information so you have the ability to contact her when you want to, but if she is not comfortable with it, at least there is the possibility of future contact by giving her your information.

F. How Do Women Turn Down Men When They Are Not Interested?

Deep down men are afraid to approach women because they are scared to death that they will be rejected, laughed at, or in some way made to look foolish. Let's face it, not every girl you approach will be interested in you. Not knowing how a girl will react is what really holds men back. If men knew when asking a girl out that the likely worst case scenario was that she would politely say, "thanks, but I have a boyfriend," we would probably be a lot less nervous about taking a chance.

So what do women generally do when a man they are not interested in asks them for their phone number? The survey responses showed overwhelmingly that they would politely respond that they had a boyfriend, even if that weren't exactly true.

Would this answer hurt? Maybe a little, but it would not be nearly as horrible as our imaginations would lead us to believe. The reality is that there are very few women in the world who are callous enough to be truly rude to someone who approaches them and expresses interest. Mostly, they will be flattered, even if they are not interested.

G. Other Surveys

The information in the survey responses should be extremely encouraging to you. Essentially, they say that in a world filled with beautiful women, a proactive, confident man has very little competition. If you just approach a girl in a pleasant, respectful way with an attitude that conveys a quiet sense of confidence you will be way ahead of 99% of the other guys.

Of course, my survey is not the only one on the subject. Other surveys have shown that women place a lot less emphasis on appearance and money than you might guess. For example, one recent survey showed the traits women found most important in a man:

Intelligent	79%
Funny	70%
Attractive	34%
Athletic	12%
Wealthy	6%

American Demographics Magazine, April, 2001.

Another survey showed how women met their past boyfriends:

Friends, coworkers, family	65%
Worked with him	36%
Met at school	27%
Met online	26%
Met at bar or coffee shop	26%
Church, grocery store	<20%

American Demographics Magazine, February, 2002.

This survey tells us that most women date men that they either already knew from work or school or that they met through a mutual acquaintance. This is not surprising given how rarely men will approach a woman that they don't know.

A survey on match.com confirmed this by asking women how often they were asked out on dates. The responses indicated that 40% of the women aged 25 to 34 had not been asked out in the past twelve months. And in case you are thinking that this must be the ugliest 40%, let me refute that with a story that appeared in the newspapers a couple of years ago.

The story was about Ashley Judd, the famous actress, describing how she had become engaged to a racecar driver. When asked why she decided to go out with him she explained that **he was the only one to ask her out in a year!**

Imagine that – a beautiful, intelligent, wealthy woman, and she goes an entire year without getting asked out on a date! Why? Because generally men are cowards about approaching women and are terrified of being rejected. But as we will discuss in detail in the coming chapters, if you can learn to control this fear, to own it and not let it control you, then you can take absolute control of your life.

24 –Take Action!

Chapter Two

Developing a Positive Attitude About Approaching Women

If you recognize the importance of women in your life and follow the steps in this book you can become more enlightened in your dealings with women. You can immediately begin to have much more enjoyable interaction with women. It is possible to stop being scared and nervous about approaching women and start having a lot more fun and success in pursuit of them.

A. The Importance of Having Women in Your Life

If you are a normal heterosexual man, then having women in your life is very important to your happiness. This is true whether you only like to date around or if you prefer monogamous committed relationships. While there are certainly some men who claim that women are not important to them, this is nonsense.

While there can sometimes be pain involved with pursuing women and with relationships, it is infinitely preferable to a life without them. How boring would life be without women to share it with? Or maybe even worse, sharing it with someone you really didn't want to be with?

It is odd to me that you will often hear men say that they aren't interested in dating around a lot but only wish to find their soulmate. This is an indication of a man with a strong fear of rejection. I mean, how are you supposed to find your soulmate if you don't date a lot of different women? Is she just going to show up in your life and you both will immediately know that you are soulmates? Of course not. But many men act as though that is what they are waiting for.

For a man to have a happy and well-rounded life, he must first recognize that women play an important role. Your goal may be to find the woman of your dreams or it may be to have many, many girlfriends. What you desire now is a personal preference and it may change as time passes, but it is important to recognize that a lot of your happiness will be determined by your relationships with the opposite sex. If you are a confident man who can pursue the women he is interested in without fear of rejection you are much more likely to find that happiness.

B. Why Men Are So Resistant to Working on Their Skills

Many men will expend a great deal of money and effort on things that are much less important to their happiness than women. They find nothing wrong with the idea of spending an entire Saturday working on their golf game, but they would be embarrassed to spend five minutes working on improving their skills at meeting women. They think that it should be innate. They could never admit to other men that they are scared to approach women and that they fear being rejected. But every man has these fears.

This is one area in our culture where men are at a serious disadvantage to women. Women talk with each other about everything having to do with men – dating, sex, what they fear, what they want, and everything else. Have you ever looked at the articles in a typical women's magazine? Nearly all of the articles will have something to do with dating, or sex, or relationships.

What about men? What kind of reaction do you think you would get if you tried to start a discussion about relationships and dating advice in the locker room at your gym? You would probably be met with a lot of blank stares. Men do not discuss this stuff, unless it is to brag about their claimed sexual exploits.

Learning how to meet women and get dates is simply not something that is taught anywhere during a man's life. It is not taught in high school or college and it is certainly not something your father teaches you. So we end up muddling through life, either getting set up with dates or asking out women that we already know. And even then we are nervous as hell about it.

Meeting women is like any other skill. You cannot improve your results without some direction and practice. This book will give you the direction and it is up to you to get the practice. The idea that you are either born with this skill or that you just don't have it is crazy. It is a learned skill just like any other. At some point in their lives Joe Montana had to learn to throw a football and Barry Bonds had to learn to hit a baseball.

Any man who is good at meeting women and getting dates has gotten that way through past experience. And any man who makes a conscious effort to improve his ability can do so.

To illustrate just how silly the notion that men do not need to work on these skills is, let's consider how most men react when they see a beautiful girl. Here is a typical scenario: a group of guys are eating lunch. Their waitress, a gorgeous girl with a beautiful figure, asks if everything is okay. They all say "great," and she leaves. They then immediately start talking about how hot she is, how they would love to date her or sleep with her, etc. But no one does anything. They leave without any of them making even the slightest effort to flirt with her, to get her number, or to let her know they are interested.

The amazing thing is that if you just take action and pursue what you want, you will often get it. This is a broad truism that applies to all areas of life, but it is especially true when it comes to meeting women and getting dates.

Unfortunately, many men who do want to improve their results with the opposite sex will have unrealistic expectations about how to make it happen. They want some kind of quick fix. Many men will pay a lot of money for things like lists of pickup lines that are guaranteed to work, or instructions on how to hypnotize a woman into wanting to have sex with you, or any number of other scams designed to separate you from your money.

What I suggest requires changing your attitude – becoming a braver, more confident man. You will be surprised at how quickly you see results after you begin to take action. If you consistently make the effort and follow the steps outlined in this book you will markedly improve your love life and begin having a great time meeting lots of women and getting many dates.

Chapter Three

The Power of Confidence

A. Why Confidence is So Important

What is confidence? Webster's defines confidence as having a strong belief in yourself and an attitude of boldness. If you truly like who you are then you are likely to be a confident person. If deep down you do not like who you are, then you will have a much more difficult time developing confidence. So if you find that you don't like yourself as much as you should, then you need to take stock of your positive and negative qualities. Spend some time thinking about your positive qualities and what a worthwhile person you are. Then spend some time thinking about what you don't like as much and decide how you will work on improving those traits.

For our purposes there is one reason why we should focus on developing confidence. Very simply, women love confident men. Ask any group of women the personality traits they find attractive in a man and confidence will always be at the top of the list. Being sensitive, thoughtful and caring are all wonderful qualities that many women like in a man. But there is no male personality trait that is in more demand than confidence. Think about it. Have you ever heard a woman describe her significant other by saying, "He is just great – wimpy, frightened, and scared of the whole world. I am crazy about him." Of course not, women want a strong, confident man.

With all of today's issues about gender equality and political correctness in the workplace, men are often confused about what women look for in men. They mistakenly think that women want men to be more sensitive and open, the kind of men who are willing to be vulnerable and to cry in front of them. While some women may want (or at least say they want) these qualities in men, what most women are initially attracted to is very different. They want strong, confident, assertive men who are not scared of the world.

B. What if You Don't Feel Confident?

What if you are overwhelmed with nervousness and you just don't feel very confident? How do you handle this? One good technique is to act like someone who is an extremely assertive and confident person. Ask yourself how you would act if you felt strong and confident, what your facial expressions would be, what your posture would be, what your voice would sound like, and anything else that you picture when you think of a confident man. Imagine what that would feel like and begin to act as though you already feel that way.

While that may sound impossible, it is not. Actors do it all the time. Tom Hanks has never personally experienced being a platoon leader or an astronaut or a gay man dying of AIDS. But he is able to imagine what it must have felt like to have been in those situations and to have those experiences. He then pretends to be that person.

You can use this technique when you want to approach a woman, but you just don't feel confident. Just ask yourself what it would feel like to be confident and then pretend that you feel that way. If you know someone you consider very confident, imagine what he must feel like and act like that. Or use a character in a movie or television show as a role model. And then walk right up to the girl you want to meet, smile, and say something. With a little practice you will begin to consistently feel this way yourself.

Here is a piece of information that should immediately raise your level of confidence. The women you approach will immediately think more of you for being brave enough to go up to them. The very act of approaching a woman will make her view you as a much more confident, attractive man.

Women know the reason that they are so rarely approached – because it takes a lot of courage to approach a complete stranger and risk rejection. So her first impression will be that you are bold and confident. This will immediately tint her view of you in a very positive way. A girl who may not have given you much thought before will suddenly see you as a strong, confident man who goes after what he wants.

It is surprising how rarely women, even drop-dead gorgeous women, are approached in places other than bars. Most women very rarely experience an actual, out-of-the-blue, sober "Hi, I just noticed you as I was ordering my coffee and you have the prettiest eyes," kind of approach. The kind of approach that will have her phoning her friends and saying, "you won't believe what just happened."

One last point on confidence. If it is just impossible for you to approach a girl without getting incredibly nervous, do it anyway. You will be amazed at how much success you have just from trying, even without being the least bit smooth. Women will admire and respect you for having courage and making the effort, because so few guys do. And the more girls you approach the more comfortable you will get and you will find yourself succeeding more and more often.

C. Myth: Women Don't Like Nice Guys

It is all too common for men to lament about how unfair it is that women love cocky jerks and are not attracted to nice guys. This is a complete misconception that arises because men confuse being nice with being a wimp. There is a huge difference.

Women have absolutely nothing against nice guys. Certainly there are a few unstable women out there who actually like to be abused and treated badly, but you would not want to date these dysfunctional women anyway. The normal, well-adjusted women that you want to date do like nice guys. They want to be treated with respect and appreciate a man who is sincere and thoughtful.

What women do not like are wimpy guys. Guys who are too scared to approach them - the kind of guy who might work for weeks or even months with a girl he is obviously attracted to, but he just can't muster the courage to ask her out. Guys who lack confidence are viewed by women as wimpy. Women see them as lacking the strength to take control of their lives and go after what they want.

Most guys who live this way would say that they are just being "nice," and that they don't want to come on too strong. In reality they are just timid, shy, and scared of rejection. These things have nothing to do with being nice and everything to do with being wimpy. You can be a nice guy without being a wimp. You can be confident and strong while still being polite and thoughtful.

Here are a few common male behaviors that signal wimpiness to women:

1. Frequently complaining about something (job, boss, relationships with other people, etc.) without ever doing anything about it.
2. Frequently talking about future plans (career, school, fitness, money, etc.) without ever following through.
3. Acting intimidated when meeting new people or in other social settings.
4. Having bad posture.
5. Being unable to make eye contact.
6. Having poor speech habits (mumbling, speaking too softly to be heard, etc.).

If you send out signals like these to women they are going to view you as wimpy, making it difficult for you to attract them. So if you have any of these habits you should work on eliminating them.

Women are attracted to confident, assertive men and are repelled by wimpy, self-doubting men. You may think this is untrue if you have personally known a woman who was totally in love with a real jerk boyfriend, but you are probably mistaken about what she really likes about him. This is a very common area of confusion. Men who are cocky jerks are often very confident. In fact, it is nearly impossible to be a cocky jerk without being confident, or at least giving off an appearance of confidence. Women are attracted to these men because they are confident. They are not attracted to them **because** they are jerks, they are attracted to them **in spite** of the fact that they are jerks. They are willing to put up with their lousy personalities because they simply cannot resist the attractiveness of a confident man.

D. Easy Going Attitude

The ideal attitude you want to develop for meeting women is one of a friendly, outgoing, and assertive guy. A happy, friendly personality can be one of the most important tools you can have in meeting and attracting women. Do not confuse a confident attitude with the attitude of an obnoxious jerk. You can be confident without being a jerk. Confidence just means that you are sure of yourself and comfortable with who you are.

E. My First Approach

Here is the story of the first time I approached a girl outside of the usual avenues (friends, bars, school, or work). I include it here only to show that any guy can do it at anytime. The only thing that you have to do is muster a little bit of courage and act. Any guy can teach himself to do the same thing.

I was at a bookstore killing time with a friend. I had no plans to make my first approach on this night, although I had been studying the subject for awhile without actually taking action.

Then I saw this beautiful girl going up the escalator. She had long, dark hair and was wearing a leather mini skirt and tall black boots. To say the least she caught my attention. With no real plan, I went up the escalator and began browsing through books on the same aisle as her. I was trying to think of something to say to her for a long time, it must have been at least five minutes or more.

Finally, I screwed up my courage and walked up to her and told her the truth. That I had been trying to think of something to say to her since I first saw her. She seemed taken aback, but I was able to introduce myself, ask her name, and strike up an inane conversation about the book she was holding.

I fumbled and mumbled my way through the conversation and the only one who seemed to be more uncomfortable than me was her. I ended up giving her my business card but left without even asking for her phone number. As far as pickups go, it appeared to be a pretty big failure. But the funny thing was that afterwards, I was completely exhilarated. I could not stop grinning. I had faced my fear and conquered it. It was totally empowering!

Ultimately she did call me and we went out a couple of times. But the most important thing was that I had defeated my own fear of rejection. I had done something that terrified me. I had approached a beautiful stranger and let her know that I was interested. I was not smooth or confident, but I still managed to overcome my biggest barrier, **fear**. I realized from that day forward I would never again allow fear to keep me from approaching a beautiful woman. And you shouldn't let fear stop you either. If you just believe in yourself and take a few chances you will be amazed at what can happen.

Chapter Four

Take Action!

In learning how to meet women, many men are looking for some magic formula that will work every time with every girl. Sorry, but no such magic formula exists. There are a million different ideas and techniques a man could use to help him do better with women. But there is not a single one that will lead to 100% success.

There is a formula that will lead to a 100% likelihood of your having success with women and getting dates. Here is the formula: you have to approach women and ask them out on dates. This sounds simple and it is, but it is not necessarily easy. Your success will primarily depend on how well you can overcome your biggest problem: yourself. You must teach yourself to ignore the inner dialogue that has always given you excuses to not approach women. You have to train yourself to take action.

That is 80% of it. The other 20% is the use of techniques that can help improve your rate of success in gaining a girl's interest; but the biggest thing is to decide to quit being a coward. If you approach a lot of women you will get a lot of dates. If you only rarely approach a woman you will only rarely get a date. If you never approach women you will never get a date. There is a direct correlation between how much you put yourself out there and how many dates you get.

You have to be willing to approach women even though you may face a certain amount of rejection. With experience you will learn what works and what doesn't work for you. With practice you will begin to succeed much more frequently than you did at first, which will encourage you to act more and more. But first and foremost, you have to take action.

A. Be Proactive

You can greatly improve your success with women through a conscious and calculated effort. You can learn to improve your ability and success with the opposite sex as surely as you can learn to invest profitably or hit a golf ball. It takes effort but if you consistently approach women you will find that you can have as many dates as you want.

A television program entitled "The Libido" that aired on the Discover Health channel included the results of an experiment conducted on a college campus. One part of the study involved a rather average looking young man who would approach girls on the campus that he did not know and immediately say to them, "Hi, I've seen you around campus and I think that you are very attractive. I was wondering if you would like to go on a date sometime?"

How often do you think the girl said yes? **50% of the time!** Success on one of every two attempts!

Even I was shocked. What more evidence is needed to convince you that if you are assertive and ask for what you want there is a very good chance you will get it.

So the statement that 'all you have to do is take action and you will succeed,' may sound like an empty promise. But it is absolutely true. If you sincerely approach ten women over the course of a week I bet you will get at least a couple of phone numbers. This is true even if you are incredibly nervous and somewhat bumbling. After you get better and your confidence grows you will succeed much more frequently, but even in the beginning you will be amazed at how well you do. You will find that you are capable of getting dates with girls that you previously thought were completely out of your league.

If you take action and begin to make meeting women a priority in your life you can have a dating life that you now only dream of. Everything else in this book is secondary. If you get only one thing from this book it should be to **act**. If you act, you will succeed. If you do not act, you will fail. This does not mean that you will get a date with every girl you approach. It doesn't mean you will succeed with 50%, or 30%, or even 10%. Different men will get different results. But it is a certainty that if you make approaching women a part of your daily life, you will have a lot more women in your life than if you do nothing.

We have all had that puzzling experience of seeing a beautiful girl with a guy who was not that handsome, or maybe even downright ugly. While working as a waiter while in college I was constantly baffled by seeing gorgeous girls out with guys that were not even slightly attractive. Sometimes this can be about money. Women are attracted to powerful men and having a lot of money is one measure of power.

Often, though, it has nothing to do with money. Sometimes it is because the man has other qualities that make him very attractive – confidence, charisma, a sense of style. But the most common reason an average guy would have a gorgeous girl is simply because he took a shot – he asked her out. It is amazing how often you can get a girl that you consider out of your league if you just took a chance. Let her know that you are interested. Sometimes that alone can make a girl become attracted to you.

B. Numbers Game

To enjoy great success meeting women you have to recognize that, in large part, it is a numbers game. Men who consistently approach women will be the ones whose lives are constantly filled with women. The more women you approach, the more phone numbers you will get, and the more dates you will have.

The extent of your success will depend on a number of factors – the impression you make on the girl, timing, her availability, and many other things. But one thing is certain: if you approach women, learn from the feedback you get and focus on improving, you will have plenty of women in your life.

The more you understand this principal the easier it will become to develop a healthy, "thick skinned" attitude about rejection. You cannot underestimate the importance of this. The greatest impediment to most men's success is their fear of rejection. Chapter Five will outline this problem in detail and address ways to handle it.

Being thick skinned is important. As you approach women you will come across some who are polite but uninterested, a rare few who are somewhat rude, and many who are absolutely flattered and want to go out with you. The important thing is that you not let the ones who turn you down keep you from getting to the ones who will be excited to go out with you. Don't let a few meaningless no's keep you from experiencing those wonderful yes's!

C. Always Be on the Lookout

It helps to be constantly looking for women you find attractive. It is not so much that you have to be constantly approaching women, it is the development of an attitude. Lets face it, if you are a normal male you do not need to work at noticing pretty girls – you can't help seeing them. What you want is to be willing and able to approach an attractive girl whenever and wherever you see her. If you do not have this attitude then when you come across an opportunity you will inevitably make excuses for not acting. 'She seems like she wants to be left alone,' 'I can't hit on her here, it's the grocery store,' or 'there's another guy standing near her, I'll seem like a goofball to him,' and on and on. Banish those excuses from your inner dialogue and teach yourself to take action whenever opportunities present themselves!

It is important to always be on the lookout for new opportunities. Think of it with a salesman's attitude. An effective salesman would not just pitch one potential client and then sit around and hope that the client will decide to buy. He would go and pitch another client, and then another. You are always better off if you have many irons in the fire.

D. Joey Tribiani as a Role Model

Anyone who has ever seen the television show "Friends" is familiar with the girl-chasing character of Joey. Upon spotting a girl he wanted to meet, Joey would approach her with an over-the-top, cheesy grin and his standard "How YOU doin'," line. As ridiculous as that delivery is, there are a couple of traits in it that are worth emulating.

First, it is sincere and candid. The message to the girl is very clear: I am attracted to you. Unlike most men, he doesn't try to hide the fact that he is attracted. His facial expression and tone of voice let her know exactly what he is thinking.

Second, it is delivered without fear. He does not wait for confirmation that she likes him before he makes it clear that he likes her. He makes it very apparent from the start. He is fearless and does not even consider the possibility of rejection.

Now I am not suggesting that you model yourself in every way after Joey Tribiani. But most men would do a lot better if we approached women with a lot more sincerity and a lot less fear.

E. Do Not Procrastinate

When you see someone you want to meet it is important to act right away and not give yourself a chance to chicken out. The more time you think about it the more likely it will become that you will talk yourself out of it. If you force yourself to approach her immediately, as soon as the thought enters your head, you will act before you even have a chance to get too nervous.

Waiting too long and thinking about it too much can ruin your chance of meeting the girl. You can pass up a million opportunities by convincing yourself that you need to wait until all the circumstances are exactly right before you take action. Every time you are too weak to pursue an opportunity you could be passing up a chance to meet the girl of your dreams! The only sane thing to do is to try to meet the girl and see how things go. If it doesn't work out, at least you tried and you can move on. It's that simple.

Chapter Five

Rejection

Why do so many men refuse to take action and pursue the very thing that they want most in life – to be with a woman they find beautiful and exciting? The answer is simple: fear. We are scared to death of being rejected and made to feel foolish.

Let's face it – fear of rejection is what stops us from approaching the women we are attracted to. We make a variety of tired, old excuses for failing to act, but that is what it comes down to. We are afraid that the girl will reject us and make us feel foolish. Understanding and dealing with our fear and then learning to embrace our role as the pursuer is crucial in learning to meet women and get dates.

A. Understanding Your Fear of Rejection

If asked most men would say that they do not have a fear of rejection. They would claim other reasons for not approaching women: they are too busy, they want to get to know a girl first, or they are not interested in "playing games," etc. Other men say they are not interested in knowing how to meet women they don't know because they are not into chasing women but are only interested in a serious relationship (although I am not sure how you get into a serious relationship without dating some women first). The sad truth is that these are just lame excuses for being too scared to take action.

If men had no fear of rejection the world would be a very different place. Men would fearlessly approach women at every opportunity. They would try things they don't even consider a remote possibility now. Upon seeing an attractive woman at the video store, or the dry cleaners, or anywhere, they would immediately approach her and try to strike up a conversation. They would tell her she was beautiful and that they wanted to take her to lunch and get to know her. Men would unhesitatingly pursue the women they wanted with passion and without any concern that they might fail. They would understand that they might as well try because they would be no worse off if rejected by the girl than if they never pursued her at all. The end result would be exactly the same – no girl. Wouldn't this be a much more rational and logical world?

But in the real world very few men behave this way. Why? Because men are scared as hell that women will reject them and that they will look foolish. It is as simple as that. Men feel like if they approach a woman and she does not immediately reciprocate her interest, then they have failed horribly and the whole world will laugh at them.

If you are still not convinced and believe that your actions are not controlled by fear, consider this hypothetical scenario: imagine you had the ability to read minds. Any time you wanted to know someone's thoughts you just zeroed in on their mind and read it like the headline on a newspaper. And the next time you walked into Starbucks you saw an absolutely gorgeous woman, a woman so desirable that you had to tell yourself to stop staring at her.   Then you read her mind and knew that she was just as attracted to you. You **knew** without a doubt that there was no way she would reject you. You knew she was holding her breath just hoping that you would come introduce yourself and ask her out.

What would you do? Would you walk away and say nothing to her? Of course not! You would confidently walk over and introduce yourself knowing that she was eager to meet you. You would boldly ask for her number because, why not, you knew she would give it to you.

Okay, so this scenario is a little far-fetched. No one can read minds and know exactly what someone else is thinking. But it illustrates very clearly how much our actions are drastically controlled by our fear of rejection. In the imaginary scenario you approach her confidently. Under normal circumstances (where there is the possibility of rejection) you walk away without saying a word – a world of difference all because of your fear.

It is not only average guys that have this fear. All men feel this way to some extent. Even men that should be overflowing with confidence are held back by this same fear.   Joey Harrington, the Detroit Lions quarterback, has described himself in interviews as very shy with women. He is a tall, handsome, multimillionaire, professional quarterback and he still gets nervous around women. If this guy can't be confident with women who can?

The answer is YOU, and me, and anyone with the proper mindset and attitude. Because meeting attractive women and getting dates is all about being confident and taking action.

Most men would agree that they would like to have a woman in their life (some would say several women) who they found sexy, intelligent, interesting, and fun. Yet when they see someone who might fit this description they are too scared to try to meet her. It would never even cross their mind to try to meet her or get her phone number. They act as though there is some kind of law against it.

Why is this? Somehow we as men have been trained to believe that when it comes to women it is more important to avoid pain than it is to pursue what we want. We have been conditioned to only pursue women when we are assured of success. We need to retrain ourselves to reverse these priorities. To understand that the "pain" of rejection is really not that big a deal and that pursuing what we really want is what life is all about. We need to realize that it is worth taking some chances to live the life that we really want to lead.

B. Dealing With Your Fear of Rejection

So how do you deal with your fear of rejection? Like most fears, overcoming it is not complicated, but it is not easy, either. First, you have to accept that your fear exists and that it has controlled your actions in the past. Second, you have to view the fear realistically and not allow it to become exaggerated in your mind. Finally, you have to control your fear so that it does not control you.

1. Acceptance

It is important that you recognize that this fear is holding you back and keeping you from having a much better love life. Accept that you are going to feel a certain amount of anxiety when you approach a girl. No matter how experienced you become you will still feel your pulse rise at this time. This is normal. There is always anxiety when facing the unknown.

As we just discussed we know that, if not controlled, fear of rejection will greatly affect your actions. We also know that your actions would be radically different if you felt that there was no possibility of failure.

Every time you approach a new girl you will have some butterflies in your stomach. Regardless of your level of experience there will always be a little nervousness. See this for what it is – a rush of adrenaline that is your body's way of telling you that you have its full attention. Do not fight this feeling. Embrace the fact that you are participating and actually living life rather than just sitting on the sidelines like most men.

The more women you approach the more comfortable you will feel doing it and you will see firsthand how rare it is that a girl is outwardly rude to you.

It is important that you not fall into the trap of thinking that this fear can be completely eliminated. That you will do this first and **then** you will begin to approach women. If you take this approach you will never act. There will always be some fear so just accept it and learn to use it to your advantage.

2. Viewing it Realistically

Before you can control your fear and use it to your advantage you must see it for what it is. You cannot let yourself mentally exaggerate it into a much bigger problem than it is. Unfortunately, most men imagine a terrible worst-case scenario and convince themselves that it will happen.

Let's examine the risk involved in an actual situation. Say you are on your way to catch a plane and see an attractive woman you would like to meet when you arrive at the gate. She is not wearing a ring and presumably available, so you sit near her and try to strike up a conversation by asking her something about the trip. You could say something like, "So, do you live in New York or are you just traveling there?"

What risk is involved with what you just did? What are the possible negative outcomes that make most men far too scared to even consider trying to talk to her? The absolute worst case scenario would be that she was kind of rude and made it clear she didn't want to have a conversation with you.

That is the absolute worst possible outcome. You will note that it did not involve loss of life or limb. If she were not interested in talking to you, a more likely result would be that she might tell you that she is traveling there to visit her boyfriend. Most of the time you will not get either of these results, but instead end up having a pleasant conversation. Do this often enough and some of the time you will end up with a phone number and a date.

If your fear is that you will get an embarrassingly rude response, put those fears to rest. As long as your approach to her is polite and pleasant, it is almost certain that you will not get a rude response. How could you? After all, how could any reasonable person be rude to someone who is being nothing but nice and polite to them? And on the off chance you did receive a rude response, big deal. If she is such an ugly person as to treat you rudely when you are just trying to strike up a pleasant conversation, then you don't need to concern yourself with her opinion.

Personally, I can only think of a couple of times when I got a response from a woman that I would consider rude. One of these was a woman I eventually dated and the other was a very drunk girl in a bar. I would gladly trade a hundred rude responses for the feeling of strength and confidence I developed when I overcame my fear of approaching women.

As unpleasant as the thought of being turned down may be, in the big scheme of things it is not a big deal. It is just some girl, someone you will probably never see again, someone who knows nothing about what a great guy you are, who is saying "no thanks." As you become bolder about approaching women, one thing you will discover is that after you have been turned down a few times it becomes much easier.

While men tend to exaggerate how bad it would be to get turned down, they also tend to exaggerate their chances of getting turned down. You will succeed far more often than you imagine if you just try. As described in Chapter Four, the on-campus study in which a complete stranger politely asked women for a date resulted in women saying yes 50% of the time. It just goes to show that if you don't let fear get in the way and you sincerely approach a woman you have a very good chance of getting what you want.

When it comes to meeting women you have to accept that there is a certain amount of risk involved. Most worthwhile things in life do involve some risk. It would be nice if we could accomplish great things without risking failure but that is just not reality. The sooner you accept that it will be necessary for you to take a few chances in order to get what you want, the better off you will be.

As crazy as it seems to be scared of approaching women, it is a very rare man who is confident enough to walk up to a woman he finds beautiful and let her know that he is interested. If you can alter your attitude and become that man you will absolutely change your life. There is no better feeling than knowing that if you see an attractive woman you have the ability and confidence to approach her.

3. Controlling and Using Your Fear

The third and final step is to gain control over your fear. When you have the proper attitude and have accepted your fear for what it really is – a minor bump in the road to getting what you want, you will easily be able to control it and use it to your advantage.

So the next time you feel nervous before approaching a girl, don't be bothered by your fear, embrace it! Understand that this is just a normal rush of adrenaline you would feel anytime you do something exciting. See how it makes you feel alive and energetic and use that rush to your advantage by seeing it as your body's way of telling you to take action!

Remember, if you approach a girl and she does not like you it is not the end of the world. It doesn't have any real meaning at all. It could be that she was in a bad mood, was having PMS, has a boyfriend, she is a very unpleasant person or, my personal favorite, she has really bad judgement.

Afterwards, you can just chalk it up as a "swing and a miss" and move on to the next opportunity. You are absolutely no worse off than if you had not tried to meet her. In fact, you are better off, because you tried to meet her which puts you in a very select group of men who actually pursue what they want instead of sitting on the sidelines.

C. Embrace Your Role

Okay, so you have accepted your fear of rejection, you have viewed it realistically and you are ready to control and use that fear to your advantage. What is next? Embrace your role as the pursuer!

Imagine how your life would change if you were to absolutely conquer your fear of rejection. If you became so thick-skinned that it was nearly impossible for you to even feel rejected?

How would this impact you? If your life is like most men, it would completely revolutionize your life. You would have **a lot** more dates than you have now and the women you date would be women you really desired, not just acquaintances that you knew you wouldn't turn you down for a date.

To develop this kind of thick skin you have to realize that it is not the end of the world to ask a girl for her phone number and have her say that she has a boyfriend or is not interested. When you are able to see that for what it is – no big deal – your life will take an amazing turn for the better. You will no longer be bound by the chains of fear and you will be able to take action based on pursuing what you want, instead of constantly attempting to avoid pain.

Men often complain that it is unfair that they are the ones to have to take the initiative. Well, get used to it. Women will almost never approach a guy. And it doesn't have anything to do with your looks, or how you are dressed, or anything else.

Why does this almost never happen? Because they are women, they are supposed to be the passive ones, the hunted, not the hunters. They have been taught that it is not their role and that the guy is supposed to make the first move.

That is the way it has always been and that is the way it will always be. You can either be bothered by the fact that you, as a man, have to be the one to risk rejection, or you can embrace your role as the pursuer. It is your choice. When you think about it, ours is a much better position. For the most part, women are in a much more passive role and have to wait for men to pursue them. We, on the other hand, get to decide who to pursue.

It is important to realize that we are living the only life that we are going to get. In the not-too-distant future we will be old men, looking back upon our youth with either fondness or regret. Try to live your life so you don't have any regrets. While most guys are content to fantasize and talk about what they would like to do, you can be a man of action.

So when the opportunity appears and you see a girl you find attractive approach her with a confident attitude. She will not laugh at you or be rude; she will most likely be flattered and probably interested. You may not always get the girl, but you can always pursue what you want. Even if you don't get the girl, you will always respect yourself more for having taken action.

Chapter Six

Become More Appealing to Women

You will tremendously improve your dating life if you just take action and begin to actively pursue the women you find attractive. In addition, you can improve your likelihood of success if you make a few minor changes that will make women find you much more attractive.

You never know when you will come across a girl you may want to meet so you need to make a habit of looking your best at all times. When an opportunity arises you want to be able to approach her, without hesitating or feeling awkward because you haven't showered or are wearing dorky clothes. This does not mean that you need to constantly wear an Armani suit or look like Brad Pitt on the way to the Oscars. It does mean that you want to be dressed appropriately and look clean and put together.

It is important to remember that when you first meet a woman she will form an opinion of you almost immediately. As the saying goes, you never get a second chance to make a first impression. If it is a bad first impression, it will be very difficult to change her mind about it later. However, if you make a good impression it will give you a tremendous advantage from the outset.

Much of her opinion will be based strictly on your appearance. The good news is that you do not need to be devastatingly handsome for a woman to like your appearance and with a little thought you can consistently make a good first impression.

A lot of her opinion will be based on things that men do not give much consideration to: grooming, your clothes, the way you carry yourself, and most importantly, your attitude. In other words, much of what goes into forming her first impression are things that are completely within your control. The following are a few of the most important areas to pay attention to.

A. Have a Confident Attitude

Your attitude is everything. At the risk of being redundant (see Chapter 3), I will again say that your ultimate goal is to develop an attitude of confidence and assertiveness. Women absolutely love confident, assertive men.

One of the best things that you can gain from working on your appearance is that you will almost certainly get a big boost in confidence. If you improve your appearance you will feel a lot better about yourself and will gain confidence. So, be willing to make the effort to work on your appearance. It will pay major dividends not only in how you look, but also in how you feel about yourself and how the world views you.

B. Pay Attention to Grooming

Women notice a lot of little things that may not seem like a big deal to us. Like keeping your fingernails trimmed and free from dirt.   Making sure you don't have nose hairs sticking out of your nostrils. Keeping your breath reasonably fresh. Trimming the uni-brow. Wearing deodorant and a good cologne (but make sure you don't overdo it). Just focus on the basics.

You should also give some thought to how you wear your hair. If you are still sporting the mullet you have worn since high school, you might want to reconsider. A recent survey on about.com showed that women clearly prefer men with shorter hair.

As far as facial hair, studies have shown that women prefer a clean-shaven man. It does not matter whether it is a beard, mustache, goatee, or two-days growth. Some women may like it but, on average, more women will like you clean shaven. A clean shaven face never goes out of style.

The most important thing about grooming is just that you pay attention to it. Before you leave in the morning look yourself over to see if there is anything that might turn off a girl if she were to closely scrutinize your hygiene. Remember, women spend a lot of time looking good for us and they appreciate a man who takes the time to look good for them.

C. Get in Shape

Your level of fitness can be a great advantage to you in how attractive women find you. This does not mean that you need to look like Arnold Schwarzeneger. A few women find freakishly muscular men attractive, but most do not. In fact a gigantic bodybuilder is actually at a disadvantage with a lot of women. They see the typical bodybuilder as narcissistic and someone who probably spends more time in front of a mirror than they do.

What nearly all women do want is a guy who is fit and healthy. No gut hanging over the pants, no excessive flab, a guy who is tone and lean. Ideally, a lean, trim guy who looks good in and out of clothes. Someone who looks like he takes pride in his appearance.

If you begin to exercise and get in shape you will not only become more attractive to the opposite sex, but you also enjoy a number of added benefits. You will have a lot more energy, develop more confidence, and probably start to enjoy the process.

But even if you don't think you will ever enjoy it, start exercising anyway. If nothing else motivates you just remember this – women love a fit guy. As an extra bonus, gyms can also be a great place to meet fit, attractive women.

D. Dress Well

It is not necessary that you throw out every piece of clothing you own and start from scratch, but you definitely want to review your wardrobe and consider what you need to upgrade. Clothes are one of those areas where you can make a major overnight improvement that can drastically increase your confidence.

Unlike men, most women evaluate a man's physical attractiveness based in large part on how well he dresses. If you approach a girl at the mall, you are a lot more likely to succeed if you are dressed stylishly than if you are wearing baggy gym shorts and a stained tee shirt.

Most men do not make a conscious effort to dress to attract women. They just pick out what they like and wear it. There is nothing wrong with doing that, but if your goal is to attract women you should dress in a way that they like. The most important thing is that you dress appropriately for the occasion.

Whatever clothes you do wear should be clean and pressed. You can wear a $600.00 Armani suit but if it looks like you slept in it you are not going to impress anyone.

As far as what style you should wear, that is for you to decide. Styles change and you will wear different clothes for different occasions, so you will need to use your own judgement. If you need some guidance you can look at magazines to give you ideas, or maybe even ask a female friend to go shopping with you.

One important note for guys over the age of 30. Please do not dress like a teenager in an attempt to look younger. You will end up looking like a middle-aged guy trying to look like a teenager. This says to the world that you are so uncomfortable with who you are that you are going out of your way to masquerade as something you are not. This is the opposite of confidence.

One of the biggest issues with clothing is the fit. If you tend to wear clothes that are too tight because you are constantly planning to get in shape, then do yourself a favor – buy some new clothes that fit well now or take your current clothes to a good tailor. Then, when you do get in shape, you can buy some more new clothes that fit your new, trimmer body. Clothes make a huge difference with women, so don't skimp.

E. Don't Get Hung Up On Your Looks

The primary focus of this chapter has been to describe ways to improve your appearance. But what if you are just not that good-looking? Should you give up all hope of meeting and dating attractive women? Of course not! Men have a tendency to believe that women think about looks the same way we do. Fortunately, that is just not true.

Women frequently become more attracted to a guy after they get to know him. This doesn't make sense to men. Most men form an opinion about a woman's physical appearance within about three seconds. Her attractiveness is right there to see. You don't need to know what kind of person she is or whether she is interesting or intelligent. She is either good looking or she is not. Certainly, other things may help you decide whether she might be someone you would want to spend time, but even if she was a terrible person and you couldn't stand being in her presence, she would still be just as physically attractive.

Fortunately for average looking men, women don't think like this. A woman might think a guy is just okay looking, but he may have a certain charisma or attitude that she finds attractive. The point is it is not necessary for you to be a classically handsome man for women to find you attractive. For most women, attractiveness has more to do with a man's attitude and his sense of style. Obviously, it helps if you are six foot three and look like Russell Crowe's twin, but you can succeed with women if you are just an average-looking guy.

If you dress well, are well groomed, and carry yourself with confidence, keep yourself in reasonably good shape, many, many women will find you attractive. Since all of these things are easily within your control, there is no excuse for not making the necessary changes to create the desired appearance.

So if you don't look like George Clooney, don't worry about it. Just look as good as you can, act confident and you will do great. A man who really makes the effort to look put together is a rarity and women will definitely notice that man.

Chapter Seven

Decide Who to Approach

Most men have no difficulty locating attractive women. They are everywhere. The real issue is to program yourself to take action and actually try to meet these women. Nevertheless, there are a few rules you should follow in deciding who to approach.

A. Rule #1 – Who You Should Approach

The most important rule is that you should only approach women you find attractive. At this point you may be asking, "Why would I pursue someone that I am not attracted to?" Well, a lot of men consistently violate this rule. They will talk themselves into asking out women they are not really attracted to, simply because they know they won't get rejected.

Doing this is unfair to both you and her. It is unfair to her because you don't really want to go out with her to begin with, she is just a risk-free diversion. Since there is no real chance that it will develop into anything serious, you are misleading her and keeping her from possibly dating someone who might actually be attracted to her. More importantly, you are being unfair to yourself because you are wasting time and energy that could be spent pursuing women that you really do want to date. Always remember to pursue what you really want – life is too short to constantly spend it trying to avoid risk.

Who should you be attracted to? Only you can decide the answer to this question. Different men have different tastes. The only thing that matters is if there is something about the woman that appeals to you. If you find her appealing, then you should consider approaching her.

Some people believe that deciding to approach a woman based solely on her appearance is too superficial; that there are many other more important traits. Obviously, there are many factors to consider when deciding who to date. Different men look for different things in women. Some men want a woman with a great sense of humor. Others want a woman who is educated and successful. Still others like women who share a common interest like sports or jogging or whatever hobby he may have.

But the one trait that all men want in a woman is that they find her physically appealing. Fortunately, this is an easy one to figure out. It may be difficult to determine if a woman is honest and trustworthy or whether she is interesting or has a good sense of humor. But you can look at her and immediately decide if you find her attractive.

I am not suggesting that you focus solely on her physical appearance to the exclusion of all the other traits that you seek in a woman. Just narrow your potential field to women that you are truly attracted to and, from this group, look for those women who have the other traits that are important to you. After you start getting a lot of dates you will learn to pretty quickly determine whether she has the other characteristics that you desire.

Something you might want to try is making a list of the qualities you find appealing in women. You should include everything from personality traits, to personal interests, to body type. That is not to say that you should only pursue women who meet every criteria on your list. You want to be flexible and pursue any woman that you find attractive; but the list can give you some insight into exactly what you find most attractive in the opposite sex.

When I was single I made such a list and while reading it a few years later I was startled at how similar my earlier description was to the woman I married. She matched almost every quality on the list, from her physical appearance, to her education, to her personality. Spending some time thinking about the qualities that are important to you will make you much more likely to look for those qualities when you are deciding who to date.

Another common trap men fall into in deciding who to pursue is to assume that a girl is taken just because she is beautiful. Every beautiful woman in the world has been single at some point, many of them for long periods of time. Some really attractive women are approached far less often than average-looking women because men are intimidated by their beauty. Even if she does have a boyfriend you might catch her at the end of a relationship or just biding her time in a bad or boring relationship. Girls will often stay in bad relationships longer than they should simply because they don't have any better options. If you give her a better option she might just jump at the opportunity.

Studies have shown that most men date women that are in their same social circles – girls from work or school or someone that they were introduced to by a mutual friend. There is absolutely nothing wrong with meeting someone this way. If there are women you find interesting and attractive in your social circles, then by all means, you should explore these possibilities.

The common problem, though, is that men feel they can **only** meet women through these traditional channels. This limiting belief will drastically reduce your pool of potential women to date. The primary purpose of this book is to get you to change your attitude and open your eyes to the possibilities that surround you. So the next time you see a beautiful girl and think, "Wow, I wish I could meet her," you will realize that you **can** meet her. You don't need an introduction, all that is required is a little bit of courage and the willingness to take action.

B. Rule #2 – Who You Should Avoid

You should never approach a girl who is wearing a ring. If some guy has made that much of a commitment to her, you should respect that and leave her alone. Even if you were able to get anywhere with her (and with a lot of women you could) she would most likely bring you far more trouble than pleasure. Far too many men get involved with married women and later regret it. With millions of available single women, why go after the ones who are already taken? Why risk the possibility that her husband or fiancée shows up at your apartment with a gun? Stick with the single ones.

That leaves a very large portion of the attractive female population as available. You will find that there are so many possible opportunities that you will not have enough time or energy to pursue them all. Remember, I did not say that you should not pursue any girl who is dating someone or is in a "relationship." She is unavailable when she has a ring on her finger. Until then, she is fair game.

Another group of women you may wish to avoid are your coworkers. A lot of people date their coworkers and many do not have any problems; but if you are going to date around, you should probably avoid workplace dating. For one thing, there is the risk of a sexual harassment lawsuit. Getting sued is no fun and could cost you your job and a lot of money. Just the allegation can ruin your career because it is usually your word against hers and it almost impossible to prove a negative. So if your career is important to you, do not date your coworkers. Obviously, different situations call for different standards. A male waiter dating a female waitress would be a lot less of a problem than the President of a company who is sleeping with his secretary.

Another problem with dating your coworkers is that even if things go well, you now have a girlfriend who you see during your free time **and** your work time. For a lot of guys that is just too much time together. Then if you stop seeing her, you still have to work with her.

Finally, a word about dating topless dancers. A lot of men spend a lot of time and money in topless bars. If you have money to burn and enjoy this sort of thing, then have at it. But remember, most of these girls are extremely jaded and this is how they make their living – they flirt with guys and make them feel good so they can take their money. Maybe you can throw around enough money to get a few phone numbers or maybe even some dates, but even then your best case scenario is that you have a stripper as a girlfriend. The more likely result each time you go to a topless bar is that at the end of the night you will walk out alone and with a lot less money in your pocket. You will have a lot better luck with women (and probably a lot more sex) if you avoid wasting your time and money in topless bars and instead focus on real girls in the real world.

C. Rule #3 – Many Irons in the Fire

Here is a very common trap that men who are beginners at pursuing women fall into. They go out, approach a few women and successfully get a phone number. They get so excited by their success or by a particular girl that they stop right there. They think, "I don't need to keep approaching women, I like this girl and I will wait and see if things work out with her."

This is a huge mistake. Maybe things will work out with her and maybe they won't, but you should not focus all of your effort and time exclusively on her unless and until you are in a committed relationship.

Here is an example of how this can work against you. Let's say you meet an attractive girl at a happy hour. You have a great conversation, she seems very interested and she gives you her phone number. You go home that evening thinking that she is the one and that there is no need to pursue anyone else. The next day you call her to try to make a date but you get her voicemail, or maybe you speak to her but she can't seem to commit to a time and she says she will get back to you. Over the next week you try to reach her several times with the same result. Finally, after a week's worth of frustration, you realize that it is not going to happen and you have to begin all over again.

Here is how to avoid this frustration. You want to have many irons in the fire. You want to continue to pursue women so that you have a lot of available options. You do not want to pin all your hopes on one girl. Don't stop meeting women, collecting phone numbers, and making dates until you are actually in a committed relationship. If you stop pursuing women every time you meet a girl that you like on the assumption that things will work out perfectly with her, then you are going to face a lot of frustration.

It is great when you meet a girl and things go well but, let's face it, at this point you really don't know very much about her. All you know is that she is attractive and you had a pleasant conversation. She could be a total flake, she might have a live-in boyfriend that she didn't tell you about, or maybe she is a drug addict or a felon. The point is that you know almost nothing about her so it is crazy to start imagining a future with her. When you get to know a girl well and you really click with her, you will know it. At that point you can stop pursuing other women if you want, but don't do it prematurely.

An added benefit to continuing to pursue other women is that it reduces your availability. This will make you more attractive to women. If you seem totally desperate to go out with her and completely available whenever she wants, she will think less of you. This may seem like childish game playing, but it is just basic human psychology – we desire that which is difficult to obtain and we are less interested in that which is easy to obtain. If she believes that you have a lot of other options, she will find you a lot more interesting and attractive. So until you are in a committed relationship you should keep pursuing women and working on having many irons in the fire.

Chapter Eight

Get Near Her

This chapter outlines how to approach a woman before you speak to her. In other words, these are the things to do before you talk to her.

There are really only two things you need to do. First, ideally you want to make eye contact with her and smile. Second, you want to physically get in a position where you can comfortably talk to her. That is all there is to it.

You will note that this is a relatively short chapter, while the chapters on confidence, taking action, and having a positive attitude take up a lot more pages. The reason for that is simple: if you can get past your mental roadblocks the actual act of meeting a girl is not very complicated. All you are doing is walking up to someone and saying a few words. Once you have convinced yourself to be unafraid the rest is simple.

A. Make Eye Contact and Smile

If at all possible, it is best to make eye contact and smile at the girl before you approach her. A smile is a nice, non-verbal way of saying hello to her and letting her know that you notice her and are interested.

Anytime you make eye contact with a girl you like you should smile at her. Not a cheesy, over-the-top smile, just a natural, warm smile as a way to let her know that she caught your attention.

Most men need to learn to be a lot more relaxed and free with their smiles when it comes to women. Consider what the typical man does when a pretty girl catches him looking at her – they will immediately turn away and pretend that they were looking at something else.

Think about how stupid this is. You see a girl you find attractive and then, when you get her attention and have a chance to make a positive impression, you pretend that you don't even know she exists. It makes absolutely no sense. The only rational reaction in this situation is to acknowledge her by smiling. She might quickly look away, but as long as you weren't doing anything rude like staring at her breasts or leering for a ridiculously long time, she will be flattered by you noticing her. Generally, women want men to think they are attractive and appreciate the attention.

B. Get Close Enough to Talk to Her

It is extremely important to get physically close enough to her so you can comfortably have a conversation. Ideally, you want this to seem as natural and casual as possible. For example, if you see an attractive girl eating in the food court at the mall you could pick a seat near her table. At the gym you could use a machine next to the girl you wanted to meet. At the grocery store you could get in line behind the cute girl you saw while shopping. The possibilities are endless, but the point is for you to give some thought to how to do it and then get in a position where you can strike up a conversation with her. As soon as you do that you are ready to break the ice with her.

Chapter Nine

Breaking the Ice

This chapter teaches you how to strike up a conversation with a woman. The biggest mistake most men make in this area is in thinking that they have to say something profound or hilariously funny when they first approach a woman. Nothing could be further from the truth. You could meet a girl and get her phone number by starting off a conversation with something as innocuous as, "so, have you been waiting long for this elevator?" What you say is a lot less important than your attitude. You want to appear relaxed and confident, someone who is completely comfortable in his own skin.

A. Think of Something to Say

Although the actual words you initially say are not all that important, you should still give some thought to what you will say before striking up a conversation. There are four basic approaches: give her a sincere compliment, bring up something topical, say the first thing that pops into your head, or use a pickup line.

1. Sincerely Compliment Her

Women love a sincere compliment and this can be one of the best ways to approach a girl. You can tell her you like her outfit, her earrings, her hair, her shoes, anything. The most important thing is that what you say has to be completely sincere.

Most women can see phony flattery from a mile away and find it insulting so make sure that you truly mean what you say. Thinking of a sincere compliment should be fairly easy if you are motivated enough to approach her. All you need to do is tell her what you find attractive about her – her hair, her eyes, her smile, the way she is dressed, or anything else that draws you to her.

Approaching a woman this way can instantly work in your favor. It makes her feel special and appreciated and it also gives her an impression of you as a very confident person. Only a confident man could walk up to a complete stranger and say something complimentary. A weak, shy, timid man would never be able to work up the courage necessary to do this.

Men will often say that they don't want to say how attractive a girl is because they don't want to come on too strong, that they would rather play it cool. This is actually just an excuse. Their real concern is their fear that she will laugh at them. That she will say "Hah! I knew you were in love with me! But I don't find you interesting or attractive at all, SO BEAT IT!"

This is a very common fear, but it is 100% wrong. First, in all of the compliments I've ever given women I've never gotten a response like that. The typical response is that she is pleasantly surprised. If you just act confident, don't fear the outcome, and be honest with her you will be surprised at how often things will work out in your favor.

A sincere compliment can often make a woman much more interested in you. It is really just human nature. A compliment makes us feel appreciated and good about ourselves. If you make her feel good about herself she will also feel good about you and want to be around you more.

As much as women love compliments, there are a couple of things you want to avoid doing. First, you want to be careful to not appear groveling. In other words it is fine to tell a woman that she is beautiful, but do not act as though you feel you are unworthy of her just because she is beautiful. Women love confident men and there is nothing confident about groveling.

Second, you want to make sure your compliment is not crude or offensive. If you are going to compliment a girl's appearance, use some discretion and be classy. Do it in a way that would not be offensive to your mother if she happened to be listening. For example, telling a girl she has beautiful eyes or even a great figure is okay. Saying she really fills out her sweater or that she has a "nice ass" is not.   Use good judgement but, by all means, tell her what you like about her.

Just in case you still need convincing that women love compliments on their appearance, let's analyze the effect of the media on the typical woman. Women are constantly bombarded with unrealistic media images of what a beautiful woman is supposed to look like. For example, consider the beer commercial with the two busty supermodels that get into a fight and end up wrestling their way into a water fountain and getting soaking wet. Both of these women are statuesque with perfect faces and bodies that don't have an ounce of fat on them, except for their size DD boobs.

How do you think this commercial makes a normal woman feel? In a word, inadequate. She's not six-feet tall, she is not completely devoid of body fat, god forbid, she might even have a pimple! So she sees that commercial and feels like she is not even close to attractive. Never mind that the actresses' appearances have a lot to do with good camera work, good makeup artists and hair stylists, and probably a substantial amount of plastic surgery.

Since they are constantly bombarded with these kinds of images it is not surprising that women, even really beautiful women, often feel inadequate. Imagine how you would feel if you were constantly bombarded with advertisements that featured men with twelve-inch penises, as though that were the norm. You would feel inadequate, just like most women do.

The point is that it is understandable that women crave compliments and reassurance about their appearance. So, if you think a girl has really pretty eyes, you should say so. If you like the way she dresses, let her know. If she has great legs and looks like she works out all the time, tell her.

2. Find Something Topical to Discuss

Another excellent approach is to notice something about her, about the situation, or anything that you can think of to strike up a conversation with her. It could be something as simple as noticing that she is wearing a University of Texas sweatshirt and asking if she went to school there. If you were at a bookstore you could ask her about the book she was looking at. In a parking lot you could say, "how do you like your Honda, I was thinking of getting one?" Sometimes you can combine the compliment and topical approaches, like asking, "your earrings are really pretty, where did you get them?" Or "your perfume is great – what is it?"

Let's say you want to meet a girl at the gym. You could ask her what she thinks of a piece of equipment she is using. You could ask for some advice on what exercises she does to get her abs so rock hard.

Sometimes you can make up something that seems topical when it really isn't. For example, if you lived in Manhattan you could ask a girl, "you look very familiar – do you run in Central Park?" If she lives in Manhattan the odds are that she has at some point, which will get you started on a conversation.

A lot of men feel awkward about looking for something to say or ask because they are afraid it will seem like they are just using it as an excuse to talk to her. Of course, this is exactly what you are doing, but there is no need to hide it. You want her to know that you are interested. So what you are looking for is anything that might help you strike up a conversation.   It is really quite easy after you get a little experience.

One trick is to worry less about what you say and focus more on saying something and trying to start a conversation. If you do this you will have a chance to meet her and it might lead somewhere. If you do nothing you will probably never see her again.

3. Say the First Thing That Comes to Mind

Sometimes you may not be able to come up with anything topical. What do you do then? Your fallback should be to just walk up to her and say the first thing that comes out of your mouth. Tell her what you are thinking, or at least the PG rated version of what you are thinking. Tell her that you were trying to think of something to say and couldn't. Or that you just lost your dog. Or that you just lied to her about losing your dog. There is absolutely nothing wrong with walking up to a girl and saying "You know, you probably hear this all the time, but you have the most beautiful hair." She'll might be a bit shocked, but she will definitely love the compliment and it might just make her take a closer look at you.

It all comes back to the need for you to say something, anything, to her. As silly as some of these examples may seem to you, if the end result is that you do not succeed with her, then you are no worse off than if you did nothing. If you do nothing you will never see her again, she will be unaware of your existence, and you will be left to wonder about what might have been. If you are like most men, this is the way you live your life. You constantly see beautiful women that you want to meet and date, but unless someone introduces you to her (and maybe even tells you that she wants to go out with you) you will be too cowardly to take action. Don't be one of those guys. Take control of your life and go after what you want. Take action.

4. Use a Pickup Line

I am not a big fan of pre-made pickup lines because they are insincere. If you repeat the same line to every girl you meet, you will eventually sound like a guy who repeats the same line to every girl he meets. When you see a girl that moves you enough to approach her, you want her to feel special. You want her to know that you found her so attractive that you could not help yourself, that you just had to try to meet her. If this is the vibe she gets from you then you will have a much better chance than if she thinks you are just some cheesy guy who is going to use the exact same line on a different girl in five minutes.

That being said, it is sometimes good to have some ideas for use as a backup in case you just freeze up and are unable to think of anything. Here are a few ideas: Did you go to _____ (fill in the name of the school you attended), you look very familiar? Do you office in _____ (fill in the name of the building where you work), you look very familiar? I've never tried _____ (fill in with name of some product in her shopping cart), is it good? I just have to tell you, you have the most beautiful _____ (fill in with some attractive trait of hers – eyes, hair, outfit, whatever). There are a million possibilities.

B. Stay Relaxed and Give Her a Chance to Be Receptive

It is best if you can keep a cool, relaxed demeanor when you approach a girl. You may be a little nervous when you first approach her, but with practice you will appear to her as calm as you are when you are talking to one of your buddies.

A girl who is being approached will often become somewhat nervous, but you can turn this to your advantage. If you remain relaxed and friendly your attitude will eventually rub off on her and she will begin to feel more comfortable. This calm demeanor will give her an impression of you as someone who is confident. Of course, cultivating this attitude will take some practice but it will eventually become completely natural to you.

Since you can expect that sometimes the girl will be a bit taken aback by being approached, it is very important that you remind yourself not to get discouraged if she isn't very encouraging at first. If you keep your cool and act as though the situation is no big deal she will eventually relax.

Generally, girls are very flattered by being approached, even if they do not show it at first. This is true even if it makes them somewhat uncomfortable, or even if they are not interested or have a boyfriend. Often, this has to do with the woman you are approaching being far more insecure about her appearance than you would ever imagine. Women, even very beautiful women, want and need constant reassurance about their attractiveness. By approaching a woman you are really saying that you find her attractive and that you are interested.

If you just give them a chance, a lot of girls will be very receptive to you. For the most part, women like to be approached. So take a shot and make something happen!

88 –Take Action!

Chapter Ten

Continuing the Conversation

What if you successfully work up the courage to approach a girl, but then have trouble either keeping the conversation going or asking for her phone number? This chapter explains exactly how to handle these situations.

A. Things You Should Do

Let's say you have approached an attractive girl and started a conversation with her. How do you keep the conversation from stalling?

The most important thing is to remember to have some fun with it. If you keep a cool demeanor she will relax and will enjoy talking with you more, which will make her like you more, which will make it more likely that she will give you her phone number. So if you can't actually **be** relaxed you want to at least try to **appear** relaxed.

A very simple way to do this is to smile. Your smile says to her that you like her and that you are a happy and easygoing person. Since most guys appear really nervous or uptight when they meet a girl, your smile will also tell her that you are confident and don't get overly anxious over things that don't deserve it.

If you find it difficult to relax, don't worry about it. Just the fact that you had the courage to approach her will give her a good first impression of you. After you have approached a few women it will become much easier and you will realize how silly it is to get nervous about it. Remember that talking to an attractive girl should be a fun, enjoyable experience. If you don't succeed with her, it is no big deal. There are a few million attractive women out there so failing with any one particular girl is not the end of the world.

Something else to keep in mind during the initial conversation is that you want to keep the subject matter relatively light. Use subjects that are easy to talk about and don't make her uncomfortable. For example, it is fine to ask questions about her school or work or what she likes to do in her spare time, but now is not the time to find out her beliefs on abortion, or to bring up how painful it was when your favorite uncle died. At this point you want to keep things fun and relaxed. There is plenty of time later to talk about all kinds of soul-searching issues later. For now, you just want her to enjoy talking with you.

If a conversation doesn't seem to be flowing naturally, one good way to extend it is to ask a lot of questions about her. You can ask her if she goes to school and where, what type of work she does and where, what part of town she lives in, does she come here often, how long has she lived here, etc. There are a million generic questions that you can ask and then there are probably another million that you can ask about her specifically. As you encourage her to talk about herself she will begin to feel more and more comfortable with you.

For example, if she is wearing a sweatshirt that says "Vail, Colorado," you could ask if she has ever been there. If she has, that leads to another group of questions you can ask about Vail. If not, that leads to other possible questions about where she got the shirt and whether she ever wants to go there.

Once you are able to get her to open up and start talking a little, make sure that you listen and actually converse with her. As you listen to her, other things will come up that you can ask her further questions about. You want her to feel that you are sincerely interested in what she has to say, not just waiting for her to shut up so you can start talking again. You want her to feel relaxed and comfortable with you.

At some point in the conversation you want to introduce yourself. You can just say, "and by the way, my name is Joe." This will probably prompt her to tell you her name, although if she doesn't you should ask her what her name is. You want to try to remember her name immediately. It helps to say her name a couple of times after you first hear it. For example, you could say, "Suzanne, that's a pretty name, Suzanne." You could also just work her name into the conversation periodically to reinforce your memory. Just make sure not to do it excessively or you will come across like a used car salesman.

If at some point you realize you don't remember her name, don't make a big deal of it, just ask her again, make a joke about how forgetful you are, and make sure that you don't forget it again.

Having a conversation with an attractive girl is just like having a conversation with anyone else. If you ask questions, listen actively, and encourage her to talk about herself, she will probably like you. The more she likes you, the more willing she will be to give you her phone number.

B. Things You Should Avoid Doing

Probably the biggest mistake men make when meeting someone new is that they focus too much of the conversation on themselves. In other words, they spend far too much time trying to impress the girl instead of focusing on how she **feels** while she is talking to you. If you pay attention to her and make her feel that you are really interested in knowing her she will be much more likely to find you attractive than if you just talk incessantly about yourself and how important you are.

This is true no matter how impressive you are. Let's say you have your own business, you are a millionaire, and you played college football. All of these things are quite impressive. But if you meet a girl and within the first sixty seconds of talking to her you manage to force all of this into the conversation she will think you are a braggart and have a huge ego. This is not what you want. If you just had a relaxed conversation with her all of these things would eventually come out much more naturally. When they do, she would be truly impressed with your accomplishments and with the fact that you are so humble about them. This is a much more impressive way for this kind of information to come out.

The most important thing to remember is that you should keep the focus on her and not force the spotlight on yourself. Remember everything that was discussed in Chapter Nine about compliments and women craving reassurance about themselves and their appearance. Well, if you spend the whole conversation trying to impress her, you will spend no time addressing her and her needs. Focus on her and she will probably like you. Focus too much on yourself and she will probably feel like you are trying to sell her something that she doesn't want.

Along the same lines, something else to avoid is outright lying. Some men will approach women and just make up whoppers about how they are professional athletes or independently wealthy millionaires. Obviously, this is a huge mistake on many levels. Aside from the fact that it is just wrong, it is almost guaranteed to backfire on you. If she has any sense at all, she will probably see right through you and immediately write you off as a loser. At best, she will think that you are bragging about yourself and will think less of you. Even if you were able to convince her of the lie you would have to work very hard to keep up the façade every time you spoke to her. As the old saying goes, honesty is the best policy.

Depending on how well the initial conversation goes, you may feel like asking her for a date and try to pin down for a specific day and time. Usually, you are better off to just ask for her phone number and try to make a date later. This will give her a little more time to think about you and how confident you were to approach her that way. If you try to get too much to soon you run the risk of scaring her off. You don't want to come across like a high pressure salesman, where she feels as though you are trying to force her to commit without giving her a chance to think about it.

C. Asking for Her Phone Number

Phone numbers are very important. It is not enough to approach a beautiful woman and strike up a conversation with her, you have to ask for her phone number. It is natural to feel a little awkward when asking for it, but you have to do it. If you have a great conversation but walk away with no way to communicate in the future, you will probably never see her again. Obviously, if you are going to go to the effort of approaching her you want to at least try to get a phone number so you can meet again.

All you have to do is say, "I've really enjoyed talking with you, I'd love to chat some more. Could I get your phone number, maybe we could have coffee sometime?" Say it in a way that makes it sound like it is not a big deal. Like most other aspects of meeting women, the more often you do this the easier it will become.

When you begin approaching women you will probably be surprised at how freely a lot of women are about giving out their number. However, some women are a little reluctant about doing this. Do not take this as a rejection or assume that she has any kind of negative opinion of you. Instead, put yourself in her shoes. These days, women have good reason for being careful. There are a lot of nuts out there and, although she probably likes you, she does not know you well enough to be certain you are not some kind of wacko.

When this comes up and she is hesitant, you can offer her alternatives like giving you her work number or an email address. As a last alternative you can give her your business card or your number and ask her to call you. You should use this as only a last option because this puts you in the position of waiting for her to call you. While often they will contact you, women have a hard time making that call. They are not used to being the one to make the first call and will sometimes procrastinate about it until finally just giving up. If possible, it is definitely preferable to get a number or email address so you can contact her.

Chapter Eleven

Practice

This chapter outlines the various practice methods that can improve your skills. Of course, the best practice is to actually get out there and try to meet women, but if you are still working on summoning the courage necessary to approach women, these exercises will help you get ready for the real thing.

A. Imagine Your Approach

Let's say you are running late on your way to a meeting one morning. You didn't have time for breakfast so you stop at a coffeeshop to at least get your caffeine. While in line you notice a beautiful woman reading the New York Times. Unfortunately, you just do not have enough time to try to meet her.

How can you use this situation to your advantage? You can use it as an opportunity to exercise your brain. Ask yourself how you would meet her if you did have the time. How would you approach her? What would you say to her? What would your attitude and demeanor be?

Do this mental exercise frequently and when real opportunities present themselves you will be able to quickly decide how to approach her.

B. Become a Friendlier Person

Becoming a more outgoing, gregarious person with people in general will help you meet women. When you are outgoing and talk to many people you will have many more opportunities to meet attractive women and you will be more comfortable conversing with them when you do meet.

You should try to strike up conversations every chance you get. When you are on an elevator with someone you could say something about the weather or about how slow the elevator is. When you are in line at the grocery store you could compliment the women behind you about how cute her baby is and ask its age. While sitting in class you could ask one of your classmates a question about how they did on the last exam.

The point is that you can practice your conversational skills with any stranger. They can be old or young, male or female, good-looking or unattractive, it doesn't matter. What is important is that you gain experience in striking up conversations with strangers. The more comfortable you become with this, the more comfortable you will become talking with attractive women.

Here is something else you can do when you are walking around. Every time you see an attractive girl make eye contact with her, smile, and say hello. You will be surprised at how many smiles and hello's you get in return. If you do this often you will become outgoing out of habit and more comfortable with approaching women.

C. Visualization

Meeting women is all about confidence and one great way to develop confidence is to visualize either past successes you have had in approaching women or even imagined successes. For years sports psychologists have had athletes do mental visualization exercises to improve their performance and confidence levels. You can use this same technique to improve your ability to meet women.

Visualization can be extremely effective because your mind has great difficulty in telling the difference between an actual experience and one that is vividly imagined. So if you repeatedly imagine a scenario where you approach a beautiful girl, have a pleasant conversation with her, and successfully get her phone number, your subconscious will eventually begin to accept it as real. In other words, you will know the event was imagined, but your subconscious will not. Consequently, you will begin to feel more confident in your ability to approach women. Visualization can be a wonderful tool to reinforce your successes or even to help build your confidence when you lack real experience.

Bedtime is perfect for this. That way it can be the last thing you think about before you fall asleep. Here is how you do it. First, close your eyes and relax. Picture yourself approaching a girl and talking to her. Imagine very specific details about the event – where you are, what color her hair and eyes are, what she is wearing, etc., so you can really picture it in as much detail as possible. Imagine her smiling back and the two of you having a relaxed and pleasant conversation. See yourself asking for her number and her gladly writing it down for you.

Another thing you can do is to imagine an actual not-so-successful event, but then replay it in your mind with some mental revisions that make it a tremendous success. Maybe you approached a beautiful girl but she told you that she had a boyfriend. You could mentally replay it so that you had a great conversation with her and she gave you her number.

If you don't have any experience with visualization it may sound pretty far out to you, but give it a try anyway. You will be surprised at how effective it is at boosting your confidence level.

D. Go to the Mall

When you are ready to make some serious attempts to meet women you should go to the mall. The mall is a great place because women love to shop. They are everywhere and there are so many opportunities to meet them. There are girls that work in the stores, women sitting in the food court, women shopping or walking around the mall, etc.

The mall exercise is quite simple. Here is how it works: you go to the mall and cannot leave until you have made at least three attempts to meet a girl. If this exercise seems forced, that is because it is. The purpose is to make you actually approach some women. There are no excuses. You can't complain that there is a lack of women to approach – they are all over the place.

So get to the mall and start approaching women. The experience you gain will help you improve your skills more than you can imagine right now. As an added bonus, you will probably get a lot of phone numbers out of it.

Chapter Twelve

Where to Meet

Where can you go to meet women? Anywhere and everywhere. Some of the best places are ones that you have probably never considered. Places like the bookstore, the coffeeshop, the mall, or the grocery store. While some of the more popular places can also be used effectively a lot of them (like bars and online dating) have a lot of disadvantages.

Here is an example of how it can work. Let's say you see a beautiful girl in the grocery store. You are in line paying and she is one line over at another register, too far away to comfortably strike up a conversation. You hope that you will both finish paying at the same time so you can say something to her as you are leaving. Unfortunately, she is still waiting in line when you finish.

What can you do at this point? Are you just out of luck? Absolutely not – you look for her in the parking lot. You can walk up to her, smile, and say something like, "Hi, I've just got to tell you, you look like you just stepped off the cover of a magazine. I mean you are really beautiful."

Does that seem too over the top to work? I can tell you that it is not. What I just described is how I met my wife. If you are willing to take some chances you will be surprised at what can happen.

As far as what places are appropriate ones to try to meet women, you want to unlearn everything that you have learned in the past. Basically, society teaches us that there are only two ways that you can meet women: either through connections or circumstances.

Girls you meet through connections are ones that you are introduced to or set up with by friends, or sometimes even blind dates. Girls you meet through circumstances are ones you met because you happened to sit next to them in a class or you work together or some other situation threw the two of you together.

Don't misunderstand – I am not saying that there is anything wrong with dating a girl that you met either through connections or circumstances. The problem for most men is that they feel limited to **only** meeting women in these two ways. Thus they have limited themselves to a very small group of potential dates. This attitude is very self-defeating. We live in a big world with a lot of available women. Take advantage of that.

You want to teach yourself to take advantage of opportunities to meet women whenever and wherever you can. If you open your eyes you will see a lot of available women to date.

A. Mall

As described in the last chapter, the mall can be a great place to meet girls. If you ask a young woman what she enjoys doing, odds are good that shopping will be very high on her list. The mall is one of those places you can go where there are very likely to be a lot of attractive women. So why not go to a place where the odds are in your favor. You can try to meet girls who are shopping, or in the food court, or you can talk to the salesgirls.

B. Bookstore

Bookstores can also be fantastic places to meet girls, particularly intelligent girls. A lot of bookstores now have coffee bars and are designed to get you to hang out. The bookstore can be an excellent and subtle place for a pickup. You can drink coffee, look at books, and you will probably see a few cute girls doing the same. You can approach these girls the same way you would anywhere else. You could ask a question about the book she is looking at or maybe just compliment her on some attractive quality she has.

C. Coffee Shop

In most major cities today you can't drive more than a few blocks without seeing a Starbucks or some other coffee shop. They have become very popular places to congregate, study, or just kill time.

Of all the possible places to meet women, the coffee shop is one of the best. It is a very relaxed setting that lends itself to easily striking up a conversation. Since you seat yourself you can choose to sit near the girl you want to meet. There are a number of topics that are easy to bring up, like what she is reading, what she is drinking, whether she is on her way to or just coming from work or school, etc.

What she is reading is one of the best subjects to start a conversation. It immediately creates a number of follow up questions and can lead to a lengthy conversation. For example, if she is reading a textbook you can ask about the class, what school she attends, when she is due to graduate, what her major is, etc.

So if you haven't started hanging out at your local coffee shop yet, give it a try.

D. Grocery Store

The grocery store is another excellent yet usually overlooked place. There is something about the grocery store that makes it a very low-key environment in which to meet a girl.

The grocery store is another place that has many built-in conversation starters. You can ask about the food she is looking at or in her cart. "I was thinking of trying that, is it good?" "Is it easy to make," etc. You can ask a question about how to prepare something. "Do you know how to cook artichokes?"

You can also tell a little about her by what is in her cart. If she has diapers and baby food, you know she has a baby. If she has enough food in her cart to feed an army, she probably has a large family. If she has only a few things and they are mostly healthy items, there is a good chance she is single and lives alone. Also, there is usually plenty of time to get a good look at her ring finger and see if she is taken.

I am a little biased since I met my wife there, but I consider the grocery store to be one of the most underrated places to meet women. You have to buy groceries sometime so you might as well use that opportunity to meet women, right?

E. Bars

If the grocery store is the most underrated place to meet women, bars have to be the most overrated. Bars are the one place where many men will consider approaching a woman they don't know. Few follow through and actually approach any women, but at least they consider it a possibility.

In reality, bars are not one of the better places for men to try to meet women. Bars have a number of negatives. They are loud, they usually contain far more men than women, the women in bars are often defensive and picky, and you are far more likely to get blown off rudely in a bar than elsewhere.

Generally, women are impressed by men who have the courage to approach them, but in bars they are used to getting approached. As a result, it is much less impressive to them when they are approached by a man.

For example, you might approach a girl in a bar and tell her that she has pretty eyes. What you don't know is that you are the fifth guy to approach her that night, so it doesn't make as much of an impression. She thinks you are just another drunk guy trying to get laid before last call. Had you done the same thing at the carwash she would have been very flattered. She might have told her friends how a complete stranger came up and told her she had pretty eyes.

Why the different reaction? Because you might be the only guy to ever approach her that way in a non-bar setting. At bars women have their guard up. They are approached so often that they become jaded and suspicious.

Another problem with bars is how badly the men outnumber the women. It is not uncommon for some bars to have a ratio of two-to-one or even three-to-one. Those are not very good odds. With the odds so heavily skewed in their favor, women can afford to be a lot pickier in bars than they would be in the real world.

A girl from your office who might normally jump at the chance to date you would probably have a very different attitude if you approached her in a bar. At the office she might be attracted to your good qualities ("he's really smart and ambitious," or "he's a really good dresser"), but at a bar she might immediately reject you for some frivolous reason ("I only like guys who are at least 6'2," or "I only like guys with blond hair").

Another problem with bars is that they are usually very loud, making it hard to hear well enough to have a conversation. This can be very frustrating and make it difficult to connect with the girl or find out much about her.

Bars are also bad places for guys who do not have really thick skin. If you go to a nightclub with the intention of meeting women and you go home with no phone numbers, you might feel like a failure. Of course, you didn't really fail, you just were unable to succeed in a very difficult environment. Nonetheless, unless you have very thick skin, this can have a very damaging effect on your ego and make you reluctant to approach women.

That is not to say that you should never try to meet women in bars, because it is certainly possible to succeed. So if you are going to go anyway, you might as well try to meet some girls or at least get some practice.

For all of the negatives, the only significant positive about bars is that there are usually a lot of available girls. Even though the male-female ratio is usually bad, you will definitely find a lot of attractive girls to meet in most bars. Most of the girls there are available and there are plenty of them, so at least it is a target-rich environment.

For guys who do want to try approaching women in bars I would offer two pieces of advice. First, don't get drunk. You can drink, just don't get drunk. Being smashed is unattractive to most girls and you end up looking like a lush. Second, don't make bars the primary place that you use to meet women. There are so many other places where you will get better results.

Instead of staying out until 3:00 a.m. on Friday night, most of us would be better off getting a good night's sleep and waking up Saturday morning without a hangover. Then you can get up, go to the coffee shop, the mall, or run your errands. While you are out and about you will run across a few girls that you can try to meet. Your odds of success will be a lot better this way than at the bars. Do this and you will soon be filling up your Friday and Saturday nights with dates rather than wasting your time in bars.

F. Online Dating

Over the last few years online dating has become tremendously popular. Personally, I am not a big fan. But millions are trying it and if it works for you, then go for it.

If you do use online dating one thing you should consider is analyzing the amount of time and effort you expend and what you are getting in return. Are the dates you are getting online with the quality of women that you want to meet? Are you getting as many dates as you want? How much time do you spend reviewing profiles and sending or answering emails?

Online dating has a lot of disadvantages, some of them very similar to the problems with bars. The process of online dating can be very time-consuming, there are usually far more listings for men than women and the quality of the women that you meet online might not be nearly as good as you would meet in the real world. Yet, in spite of these frustrations, men continue to use online dating and it gets more and more popular every year.

One problem with online dating that makes it similar to bars is that, because there are so many more men than women participating, the women become much pickier than they are in the real world. They can go down their checklist and eliminate any guys who don't meet all the criteria on their "wishlist" (tall, rich, specific hair color, specific eye color, etc.). If you don't match all the criteria you never have an opportunity to meet face-to-face. Thus, you are eliminated before you can impress her with your confidence and charm, traits that don't come through on email or an online dating profile.

Why is it that online dating has become so popular? My theory is that men who use online dating are motivated by the same thing that keeps them from pursuing the women they really want: fear. In the online world you do not risk face-to-face rejection in the same way you do in the real world. You can email a girl and if she never replies, while you might be somewhat disappointed, you will have avoided the pain of a direct rejection. And avoiding pain is a good idea, right?

Wrong. If you want to get what you want out of life you are going to have to take some chances. You will be a lot better off facing up to that and dealing with it instead of looking for ways to avoid it. If you want to make an impression on a woman you will have to do something that will make an impression on her. Confidently approaching her and letting her know you are interested will make you stand out from other men. Sending her one of the thirty daily emails she receives from her match.com profile will not.

G. Dance Classes

Dance classes are a great way to meet girls. I did not figure this out until after I already had a serious girlfriend. She wanted to learn salsa so we signed up for classes. I always assumed that you had to bring a partner to these classes. It turns out that the class was mostly made up of singles, including some very attractive females. And in most of the classes you change partners frequently so you get to meet a lot of these girls.

If I had known about this when I was single, I would have signed up for so many classes I would probably have become the greatest dancer since Fred Astaire. Being a good dancer can also help you because girls love to dance when they are out. The guys that can dance have a major advantage over non-dancers because their ability catches women's attention. Even girls who are not very good love to dance with a man who is a great dancer.

I will never forget this guy I saw at a salsa club one night. He was probably in his mid-forties, short, not particularly handsome, but he was an incredible dancer. He danced with every good-looking girl in the club. Women love a man who knows how to move.

H. Traveling and Airports

Guys that travel a lot have many great opportunities to meet women. There is a lot of idle time, sitting at the gate at the airport, sitting on the plane, etc. All of this time can be put to good use.

For example, the next time you arrive at the gate to wait for your flight look around to see if there are any girls you might want to meet. When you find one you like, pick a seat near her, preferably one where it would be natural for you to have a conversation. In other words, you are not having to twist your neck or contort your body to talk to her. After you sit down you can try to strike up a conversation. This should be an easy conversation to start because you already have something in common – you are both traveling, quite possibly to the same location.

I. Gyms and Aerobics Classes

Gyms can be another good place to meet a women. You can ask a question about how to use a particular machine or how to work a particular body part. Or, since you usually see the same people at the gym, you can just introduce yourself and say that you had seen her before and wanted to say hello.

If you want an environment that is predominantly female, try going to an aerobics or yoga class. If you are not used to them, aerobics and yoga classes can be a real challenge, so be prepared. These classes are also places that lend themselves to asking questions as a way to strike up a conversation. You will also repeatedly see the same people in the same class so you can just introduce yourself and say hello.

J. Your Regular Routine

Try to incorporate meeting women into your normal routine. For example, if you like to jog at a local park you could try to meet girls there. Joggers at your local park can be good to try to meet for several reasons. A lot of female joggers are single and available which is why they jog in the first place, to stay in shape and look good. You also have a common interest (running and fitness) so you have a million easy icebreakers. You can ask how far they are running, do they come to that park a lot, talk about the weather as it relates to running - "it's humid as hell," etc. Starting a conversation is as simple as saying something like, "You look familiar, don't you workout at such-and-such gym?" If she runs there's a good chance that she also works out, maybe even at your gym. She may say no, but it could be the beginning of a conversation.

"No, I work out at the 24 Hour on Main Street."

"Really, I've heard that is a nice gym. I've never been," and on and on.

The most important thing about where to meet girls is that you don't focus too much on the location. Once you develop the proper attitude you will have an open mind and will constantly be looking for opportunities. While you are buying a cup of coffee, picking up your dry cleaning, on the elevator, at the mall buying a pair of shoes – any of these can be great places to meet a girl. Where you do it is unimportant. What is crucial is that you take action.

116 –Take Action!

Chapter Thirteen

Examples

This chapter provides some sample dialogues that are designed to give you some examples of how conversations might go. You should not try to use them as scripts or memorize them, but instead use them to give you ideas that you can build from.

A. Eating Lunch – Cute Waitress

Here is a typical situation that you might encounter. You are having lunch with some friends and being served by a cute waitress ("Jennifer"). You have already asked her name, introduced yourself and have talked enough with her to make it clear that you are trying to flirt with her. After paying the check you tell your friends that you will catch up with them in the parking lot and you wait at a place where you know she will walk past. When she appears you say, "Hey Jennifer, I was just about to leave and I just wanted to say I enjoyed talking with you before."

Jennifer: Thanks, yeah, me too.

You: I was wondering if you would like to get together for lunch sometime?

Jennifer: Well, we only just met . . .

You: I know its kind of weird since we just met, but I have this feeling that we would really get along – I tell you what, why don't we exchange numbers and we can chat for awhile and get to know each other better. Here's my card.

Jennifer: Okay

You write down her number and say goodbye.

If you think that it is never this easy and that girls never give their phone numbers to a stranger, you are wrong. Often it is just this easy. The only way to find out is to ask.

If she had been reluctant to give you her number the best response would have been to keep the atmosphere light. Possibly you could have made a joke like, "Well, I guess I am just going to have to keep eating here every day until you change your mind." Then, who knows, maybe you go there a few days later and she does change her mind. At times you might meet some initial resistance, but then, after she has had a little time to think about it, she warms up to the idea. As always, you never know until you try.

B. Coffee House

Here is another situation that you could frequently encounter. You are waiting in line at Starbucks when you notice a pretty girl sitting alone and studying an accounting textbook. You could get your coffee, sit near her and try to strike up a conversation. It might go something like this:

You: Excuse me, I couldn't help noticing your accounting textbook. I had that class when I was in college and hated it. How do you like it?

Her: Oh, I can't stand it, but I have an exam coming up so I have to study.

You: So how is the studying going?

Her: Okay I guess, but I'm getting sick of it.

You: Where do you go to school?

Her: City College, what about you?

You: I graduated from State. My name is John, by the way. And you are?

Her: I'm Sabrina.

*The conversation continues with you asking her questions about what year of school she is in, whether she lives nearby, how long she has lived here, if she comes to this coffeehouse much, etc.

You: Well, I have to get to work. You know, I've really enjoyed talking with you.

Her: Yeah, me too.

You: I'd love to talk with you again, maybe we could meet here for coffee. Can I get your phone number and we can talk again later?

Her: Sure.

After you get her number you say goodbye and go on your way.

Although this was discussed in detail in Chapter 10, it bears repeating. Even though you may feel awkward asking for her phone number, it is absolutely crucial that you ask. If you don't ask for it you will probably never see her again. If she is reluctant, you can ask for her email address or, as a last ditch effort, give her your phone number or business card and ask her to call you. But you have to at least try to get that phone number or all your effort will be for nothing.

C. Salesgirl at Mall

Malls are absolutely filled with attractive women and are great places to meet women. In our next example, let's suppose you notice an attractive woman working at the woman's perfume counter in a department store. You also notice that she is not wearing a ring. It could go something like this:

You: Hello, how is your day going? Staying busy?

Her: It's a little bit slow today. Can I help you find something?

You: I actually don't use a lot of perfume, is there a particular fragrance you would recommend for me?

Her: (laughing) I might have something that would bring out your feminine side.

You: I'm not sure that would be a good thing. Actually, I have to admit I just wandered over here because I wanted to meet you. I noticed your eyes as I was walking by. You have really striking eyes. You probably hear that a lot.

Her: Thank you, that's really nice.

*You continue the conversation by introducing yourself and getting her name, asking questions about how long she has worked there, whether she likes it, if she is from that city, etc.

You: Well, I should finish my shopping. I've really enjoyed talking with you, I'd love to chat some more sometime, can I get your phone number?

Her: I'm actually dating someone right now . .

You: Oh, are you in a serious relationship? (remember, she isn't wearing a ring so you know that she isn't married or engaged)

Her: I don't know if I would call it serious, but . .

You: That's cool, I understand if you aren't comfortable giving me your phone number right now. How about I give you my phone number and you can call me if you feel like talking or meeting for coffee or something.

Her: Okay, that would be good.

You: Here's my number and I really hope you call, I'd love to talk to you again.

Her: Okay, I'll do that.

There are a couple of things to note about this exchange. First, the use of humor is very helpful and will help create the relaxed atmosphere you want. The joke was nothing hysterical, just a lighthearted comment intended to put her at ease. Do not feel like you have to force yourself to make a joke, but if you think of something amusing feel free to say it. It doesn't have to something tremendously funny, just a mild joke is fine.

Also, if she mentions having a boyfriend, do not give up. Often, girls have boyfriends but do not consider themselves to be in committed relationships. Remember the rule – if she isn't wearing a ring you can assume it is not all that serious until she tells you otherwise.

When she hesitated about giving out her number, you could have instead asked for her email address. Since she acted like her reluctance was because she had a boyfriend, the more conservative approach is to just give her your number and encourage her to call you. While it is always preferable to get her number, you will be surprised at how often the girl will call you. She may think about your bold approach and become intrigued. Maybe that evening after work she will go out with her boyfriend on their usual Saturday night "date." Unfortunately for her, his idea of a date is for the two of them to hang out with his obnoxious roommates and drink beer. When her boyfriend ignores her complaints about their boring social life for the hundredth time, she might decide to call and see if going out with you would be a little more exciting.

D. Bookstore

If you like to meet intelligent, well-read women, the bookstore is a fantastic place. Most bookstores also have coffee bars, making them ideal places to hang out for a couple of hours. Bookstores also have their own built-in icebreakers. You can see what kind of books she is browsing which will give you material to use for a topical opening. Bookstores are very laid back, making them a great place for a casual, light conversation, the best kind for initiating contact with a girl.

In this example you are at a Barnes and Noble when you notice a beautiful girl looking through the psychology section. You casually begin to browse through books in the same general area for a minute or two. As discussed earlier, there are a lot of subtle ways you could strike up a conversation with her, but to change the pace a little, lets describe a more direct approach:

You: Have you ever read anything by _____(the name of author of the book she is looking at)? I have heard he is very good.

Her: Actually, no. I just picked this up and was looking through it.

You: (smiling) Okay, I have a confession to make. I have never actually heard of that author before, I just said that because I wanted to meet you and couldn't think of anything else to say.

Her: Really . . .

You: Yes, I have to be honest, I noticed you when you walked past because you have the most beautiful dark hair and I just really wanted to meet you. I'm John by the way.

Her: Thank you, that's very nice. I'm Susan.

You: It is nice to meet you Susan.

Her: You too.

You: Are you just killing time on a Saturday afternoon like me?

Her: Yes, I'm actually supposed to meet a girlfriend at the mall to go shopping and I had a little extra time.

You: Shopping at the mall with a girlfriend, that is like a girl's weekend tradition, isn't it?

Her: Pretty much, we do it pretty often.

You: So what do you do for a living Susan?

Her: I'm in sales.

You: What do you sell?

Her: pharmaceuticals

You: Oh, so you're a drug dealer – just kidding, I'm sure that is about the millionth time you have heard that joke.

Her: (smiling) Actually that makes it a million and one.

*You continue the conversation by asking questions about how long she has been in that line of work and how she likes it, how long she has lived in that city, etc.

You: I've really enjoyed chatting with you, Susan. I would love to talk with you some more some time. Maybe we could meet and have coffee?

Her: Yeah, maybe so.

You: Can I get your number and we'll talk more and make plans later.

Her: I don't usually give my number out.

You: I understand, I know we just met. I tell you what, why don't we exchange email addresses and then we can chat online awhile and get to know each other better. Then maybe we can meet up later.

Her: Okay, sure.

It is very important to not get discouraged or feel rejected if a girl does not want to give you her phone number. There are a lot of reasons why she may not want to give it out and most of them have nothing to do with you. For example, she might be dating someone. She could be interested in you (and losing interest in him), but does not want you to call when he might be around; but on the other hand she does not want to scare you off by telling you that she has a boyfriend.

Also, note that in this conversation you did a lot more of the talking. When you are this direct the woman will likely be a little startled and somewhat quiet at first. Do not interpret this as a lack of interest. If you do it with class, a direct compliment can be a great way to meet a girl. Everyone likes to hear compliments about their appearance. Just be aware that you will probably need to carry the conversation for awhile as she becomes a little more comfortable talking with you.

E. Airport

For guys that travel a lot, airports can be fantastic places to meet women. Women at the airport are often professionals and traveling for work, so if you like intelligent, successful women, this is a great place.

The airport is another place that has its own set of ready-made icebreakers. Everyone there is traveling somewhere and is waiting for an airplane with nothing much to do. So there are all kinds of possible topics of conversation.

In this scenario you arrive at the gate and notice a pretty woman in a business suit waiting at the same gate. There are a few available seats within conversation range of her, so you take a seat facing her. You settle in and begin flipping through your magazine. After a while you make eye contact with her.

You: So are you going to Chicago, too?

Her: Uh-huh.

You: I forgot to ask when I checked my bag, do you know if we are supposed to depart on time?

Her: Yeah, they said we're supposed to start boarding at 11:20.

You: That's good. Are you from Chicago or are you just taking a trip there?

Her: No, I'm from here, it's just a business trip for a few days.

You: Really, have you been before? Chicago is a really fun town if you know where to go.

Her: A couple of times, but I usually just end up in meetings and then hanging out at my hotel.

You: Chicago has a lot of great clubs and restaurants downtown. Also, if you are into museums it has some of the best in the country.

Her: Are you from there?

You: No, I've just been several times. I actually live here also.

*You continue the conversation by introducing yourself and getting her name, asking questions about what type of work she does, what part of town she lives in, where she is from, where she went to school, etc.   As it gets near the time to board the plane, you make sure to ask for her number.

You: I would love to show you a little bit of Chicago if you have a free evening while you're there.

Her: That would be nice.

You: Here is my cell phone number. Why don't I get yours and we can make plans for tomorrow night?

Her: Great, I'll finally get to see a little bit of Chicago.

In this scenario, it was important to not wait too long to ask her for her number. An easy mistake to make would be to wait, thinking that there will be plenty of time since you are going to be on the same flight and arriving at the same city.

However, you never know what will happen. It is unlikely that your seats will be close enough to have a conversation. You might try to switch seats if one is available next to her, but this might not be possible. Upon arrival she might be met by several people, making it much more awkward to try to have the "ask-out" conversation. So the best move is to ask her when the opportunity presents itself, rather than procrastinate for no good reason. Remember, the only reason we ever procrastinate about asking a girl out or for her phone number is that we are scared and we are trying to delay the possible pain of rejection. If you can put aside your fear, you will find that you often get what you want.

F. Advanced Example

It pays to be creative when you are thinking of ways to meet women. For the truly bold man there are all kinds of possibilities. For example, you might board a mostly empty airplane and spot a pretty girl that you would like to meet. Unfortunately, she is on row 12 and your seat is on row 14. What can you do?

Well, what is to keep you from sitting down next to her? If the plane is mostly empty the odds are that no one will show up to claim the seat that you took. And if they do, it probably won't happen until you have already chatted with her for awhile and you can just say, "Oh gosh, I must have taken the wrong seat by accident." Then later, while you are getting your luggage, you can approach her and confess that you really knew that it wasn't your seat, but she was so cute that you just had a crazy impulse to sit next to her and meet her.

This is just an example and you may never have this exact situation arise, but it is this kind of creative thinking that will give you plenty of opportunities to meet women.

Conclusion

If you get only one idea out of this book, I hope it is this: you must take action to meet women.

The difference between success and failure in meeting women is not the knowledge of some secret technique. There are a million different ideas you can use to help you meet women. You can't use all of them and there is not a single one that leads to 100% success. But there is one thing you can do that will undoubtedly lead to your success – **consistently take action!**

You have to approach women and let them know that you are interested, even if sometimes you get rejected. You have to keeping approaching women because this is how you will learn what works and what doesn't work. You will develop your own style and begin to have success and your confidence will grow exponentially. Before you know it, you will be approaching women out of habit.

The importance of taking action cannot be overstated. You can be the best looking guy in the world but if you do not take action you will not meet women. You might get a few dates here or there, maybe even a girlfriend. But you will never be in control of your romantic life. You will be waiting for things to happen to you, instead of **making** things happen. If you don't take action you are not selecting the woman of your dreams; you are simply waiting for fate to select a woman for you.

If the idea of not controlling your own future bothers you, don't worry. There is something that you can do about it. You can take charge. You can decide who you want to be with, rather than just ending up with some girl that circumstances threw at you.

Every day you probably see two or three, or maybe twenty pretty girls that you would like to meet. If you follow the advice outlined in this book and start approaching these women you will increase your confidence, get hundreds of phone numbers, many dates, have a lot of fun and maybe meet the woman of your dreams.

So the next time you see a girl you want to meet, take action! Get near her and say something! Make a habit of this and I guarantee that it will change your life.

Appendix

The following are the survey questions and a summary of the responses:

SURVEY ON WOMEN'S VIEWS ABOUT MEETING MEN

1.   Do you believe that men should be bolder about approaching women they are attracted to?

> Yes   82%
> No   18%

2.   At which of the following places would you feel comfortable if you were to be approached by a man who wanted to meet you? Which places would be uncomfortable? Mark the places you would feel comfortable with a "Y" and the places that would make you feel uncomfortable with a "N." (the percentages given are for the "yes" responses)

coffee shop	88%	wedding	88%
grocery store	41%	mall	53%
bookstore	76%	gym	55%
park	51%	concert	71%
car wash	25%	school	86%
video store	47%	work	53%
library	73%	bar	61%
dry cleaners	37%	elevator	33%
on street	22%	airport	51%
dance class	71%	church	69%

3. If a man was attracted and wanted to meet you which of the following would be the best way for him to approach you before he introduced himself? Place an "X" next to the one you would be most receptive to.

    22% a. give you a compliment
    32% b. make idle chit chat
    38% c. say something funny
    8%   d. pretend that he knows you from somewhere

4. When you meet a man what determines how attractive you initially think he is? Rate the following in order of importance from one to five, with "1" being most important and "5" being least important in deciding how attractive he is. (The responses listed are a ranking of the most popular answers)

    #3   a. how well he is dressed
    #2   b. how well he is groomed
    tie-#4 c. how tall he is
    tie-#4 d. how good a body he has
    #1   e. how handsome his face is

5.   What if you were interested in a man you just met? Place an "X" next to the one you would be most likely to do:

10%   a. give him your home phone number
56%   b. give him your cell phone number
0%   c. give him your work phone number
8%   d. give him your email address
26%   e. get an email address or phone number from him

6.   What makes a man sexy/attractive to you?

The recurring themes were confidence and sense of humor.

7.   What was the worst approach from a man that you have ever encountered?

The recurring themes were vulgar comments and cheesy lines, like "is there a mirror in your pants, because I can see myself in them."

8.   What was the best approach from a man that you have ever encountered?

Many had nothing to tell. The descriptions given by the ones who had experienced a good approach were nothing out of ordinary. For example, a guy walking up and saying something complimentary.

9.   If a man asked for your number and you were not interested, how would you turn him down?

Most said they would politely say they were not interested or lie and say they had a boyfriend.

ONLINE NEWSLETTER

If you are interested in receiving our free newsletter with tips and discussions of how to improve your success with women, please visit our website at:

www.dating-pickup-lines.com

The website and newsletter provide a lot of additional useful information that will help you have an enjoyable dating life. Your email address will never be sold or spammed.

ORDER FORM

To order additional copies of <u>Take Action!</u> <u>How to Meet Women and Get Dates</u>, please visit www.dating-pickup-lines.com or fill out and return this form with your payment to:

Personal Development Publishing
Post Office Box 27424
Houston, Texas 77227

Quantity Ordered   Price   Total

_____   @ $19.95 = $_____
+ shipping and handling$5.00/book $_____
        = Net Total $_____
+ If Texas resident, add 8.25% tax = $_____

= Total $_____

Ship To:

Name: _____
Address: _____
City, State, Zip: _____
Telephone: _____
Email: _____

*shipping to U.S. addresses only. For international shipping send email with details to: orders@dating-pickup-lines.com

(continued on back)

If paying by check, allow additional ten days for delivery. To pay by Mastercard or Visa, please fill in the following:

Exact name on account: _____

Account number: _____

Expiration date: _____

Account address if different from shipping:

_____

Signature and Date

_____

*I authorize the above-described charge to my account.

ORDER FORM

To order additional copies of <u>Take Action!</u>
<u>How to Meet Women and Get Dates</u>, please
visit www.dating-pickup-lines.com or fill out
and return this form with your payment to:

> Personal Development Publishing
> Post Office Box 27424
> Houston, Texas 77227

Quantity Ordered   Price   Total

_____   @ $19.95 = $_____
+ shipping and handling$5.00/book $_____
          = Net Total $_____
+ If Texas resident, add 8.25% tax = $_____

= Total $_____

Ship To:

Name: _____
Address: _____
City, State, Zip: _____
Telephone: _____
Email: _____
*shipping to U.S. addresses only. For
international shipping send email with details
to: orders@dating-pickup-lines.com

(continued on back)

If paying by check, allow additional ten days for delivery. To pay by Mastercard or Visa, please fill in the following:

Exact name on account: _____

Account number: _____

Expiration date: _____

Account address if different from shipping:

_____

Signature and Date

_____

*I authorize the above-described charge to my account.